Advanced Analytics and Artificial Intelligence Applications

Edited by Ali Soofastaei

Published in London, United Kingdom

IntechOpen

Supporting open minds since 2005

Advanced Analytics and Artificial Intelligence Applications
http://dx.doi.org/10.5772/intechopen.78899
Edited by Ali Soofastaei

Contributors
Maricela Bravo, Roman Mora Gutierrez, Luis Fernando Hoyos-Reyes, Rich Lee, Man-Ser Jan, Dao Huu Hung, Phan Chau Phuc Thinh, Bui Thi Xuyen, Nguyen Do Trung Chanh, Mimura Daisuke, Antoine Bambade, Kesheng (John) Wu, Octavian Dumitru, Gottfried Schwarz, Mihai Datcu, Fabien Castel, Jose Lorenzo, Ali Soofastaei

First published in London, United Kingdom, 2019 by IntechOpen
IntechOpen is the global imprint of INTECHOPEN LIMITED, registered in England and Wales, registration number: 11086078, 7th floor, 10 Lower Thames Street, London, EC3R 6AF, United Kingdom
Printed in Croatia

British Library Cataloguing-in-Publication Data
A catalogue record for this book is available from the British Library

Additional hard and PDF copies can be obtained from orders@intechopen.com

Advanced Analytics and Artificial Intelligence Applications
Edited by Ali Soofastaei
p. cm.
Print ISBN 978-1-78984-638-6
Online ISBN 978-1-78984-639-3
eBook (PDF) ISBN 978-1-83962-770-5

Meet the editor

Ali Soofastaei leads innovative industrial projects in the field of artificial intelligence (AI) applications to improve safety, productivity, and energy efficiency, and to reduce maintenance costs. He holds a Bachelor of Engineering in Mechanical Engineering and has an in-depth understanding of energy management (EM) and equipment maintenance solutions (EMS). The extensive research he conducted on AI and value engineering (VE) methods while completing his Master of Engineering also provided him with expertise in the application of advanced analytics in EM and EMS. Dr. Soofastaei completed his PhD at the University of Queensland in the field of AI applications in mining engineering where he led a revolution in the use of deep learning (DL) and AI methods to increase energy efficiency, reduce operation and maintenance costs, and reduce greenhouse gas emissions in surface mines. As a Postdoctoral Research Fellow, he has provided practical guidance to undergraduate and postgraduate students in mechanical and mining engineering and information technology. In the past 15 years, he has conducted a variety of research studies in academic and industrial environments. He has acquired in-depth knowledge of energy efficiency opportunities, VE, and advanced analytics. He is an expert in the use of DL and AI methods in data analysis to develop predictive, optimization, and making decision models of complex systems. Dr. Soofastaei has been involved in industrial research and development projects in several industries, including oil and gas (Royal Dutch Shell); steel (Danieli); and mining (BHP, Rio Tinto, Anglo American, and Vale). His extensive practical experience in the industry has equipped him to work with complex industrial problems in highly technical and multidisciplinary teams. Dr. Soofastaei has more than 10 years of academic experience as an assistant professor and leader of global research activities. Results from his research and development projects have been published in international journals and keynote presentations. He has presented his practical achievements at conferences in the United States, Europe, Asia, and Australia.

Contents

Preface

Computers and machines were developed to reduce time consumption and manual human efforts to complete projects efficiently. With fast-growing technologies in the field, we have finally reached a stage where almost everyone in the world has access to these high technologies. However, this is just a starting phase because future development is taking a more advanced route in the shape of artificial intelligence (AI). Although AI is under the computer science umbrella, nowadays there is no field unaffected by this high technology.

The overall aim of using intelligence learning methods is to train machines to think intelligently and make decisions in different situations the same as humans. Previously, machines were doing what they were programmed to do, but now with AI, devices can think and behave like a human being.

High-tech giants like Apple, Google, Microsoft, Deloitte, and IBM are highly involved in research to develop the knowledge that has started to produce innovative transformation. Although it is going to form our future, we need to know how it is affecting our work and lifestyle. So, this book has been published to give you a glimpse of the applications and advanced analytics of AI in different fields.

Structure of the book

This book contains six applications of advanced analytics and AI in different industries. All the information is supported by practical examples and scientific detail. The chapters contain enough information for both beginners to become familiar with high technologies and science applications to solve business problems and advanced readers to acquire more detailed technical information.

In Chapter 1, an introductory review briefly gives a background to advanced analytics and AI applications to help industries make better decisions to optimize processes and reduce cost.

Chapter 2 is about using a bio-inspired hybrid algorithm for web services clustering. This chapter is written by researchers from the Autonomous Metropolitan University. In recent years, methods inspired by nature using biological analogies have been adapted for clustering problems, among which genetic algorithms, evolutionary strategies, and algorithms that imitate the behavior of some animal species have been implemented. In this chapter, researchers investigate how biologically inspired clustering methods can be applied to clustering web services and present a hybrid approach for web services clustering using the Artificial Bee Colony algorithm, K-Means, and Consensus. This hybrid algorithm was implemented and a series of experiments were conducted using three collections of web services. Results of the tests show that the solution approach is adequate and efficient to carry out the clustering of large groups of web services.

In Chapter 3, researchers from the Institute of Applied Economics, National Taiwan Ocean University, explain their achievements using optimization problem analysis for smart material planning. Mostly addressed is the concept of smart manufacturing, which is based on how to effectively facilitate production activities by using automation equipment; however, causing fluctuation in production may frequently root to the uncertain incoming sales orders. These uncertain factors may be determined by economic parameters, such as the changes of trading regulations and rivals' innovations, which require to be further deciphered to reduce risk and close the gap between forecasted and actual demand. This study presents a clear operable step-by-step framework to manage and cushion the impact of uncertain external factors. It also introduces three novel and feasible production planning models by considering the economic parameters.

Chapter 4 is related to the medical application of AI. In this chapter, a deep learning-based recommendation system for aesthetic surgery, composed of a mobile app and a deep learning model, has been proposed. Researchers from the Data Science Laboratory, FPT Software Japan Co., offer the deep learning model based on the dataset of before- and after-surgery facial images that can estimate the probability of the perfection of parts of a face. In this study, scientists focus on the two most popular treatments: rejuvenation treatment and eye double-fold surgery. In the project presented in this chapter, the researchers preliminarily achieved 88.9% and 93.1% accuracy on rejuvenation treatment and eye double-fold surgery, respectively.

Chapter 5 is written by a research group at the Department of Applied Mathematics in École Polytechnique. École Polytechnique is the only Grande École among all French universities and engineering schools with separate academic departments for pure and applied mathematics. The Department of Applied Mathematics focuses on the links between the many applications and all the major fields in science, engineering, and social sciences. The title of the chapter is "Assessment of the prediction quality of VPIN." VPIN is a tool designed to predict extreme events like flash crashes. Some concerns have been raised about its reliability. In this study, the researchers assess VPIN prediction quality (precision and recall rates) of extreme volatility events, including its sensitivity to the starting point of computation in each dataset. They benchmark the results with those of a "naive classifier." The test data used in this study contain five and a half years' worth of trading data of the five most liquid futures contracts of this period. The researchers found that VPIN has an unfortunate "flash crash" prediction power with the traditional 0.99 decision threshold. Increasing the decision threshold does not significantly improve overall prediction quality. Nevertheless, they found that VPIN has a more interesting predictive power for flash events of lower amplitude. Finally, the completed research showed that, for practice, the last bar price structure is the least sensitive to the starting point of computation.

Chapter 6 is about the application of AI in Earth observation. This chapter describes a Copernicus Access Platform Intermediate Layers Small-Scale Demonstrator, which is a comprehensive platform for the handling, analysis, and interpretation of Earth observation satellite images, mainly exploiting big data of the European Copernicus Program by AI methods. The main two components in Earth observation, namely data mining and data fusion, are detailed and validated in this study. The most important contributions of this chapter are the integration of these two components with a Copernicus platform on top of the European DIAS system for large-scale Earth observation image annotation, and the measurement of clustering and classification performances of various Copernicus Sentinel and third-party mission data. This chapter is related to the completed research at the Remote Sensing Technology Institute, German Aerospace Center.

This book tries to give readers a better vision of advanced analytics and AI applications in different areas, and the authors hope that this volume will be a valuable resource for industry professionals and researchers. The presented chapters in this volume signify the state of the art regarding critical topics in advanced analytics and AI. The breadth of coverage and the depth in each of the sections make it a useful resource for all managers and engineers interested in the new generation of a data analytics applications. Above all, the editor hopes that this volume will spur on further discussions on all aspects of advanced analytics and AI applications in different industries.

Ali Soofastaei
Artificial Intelligence Center,
Vale,
Brisbane, Australia

Chapter 1

Introductory Chapter: Advanced Analytics and Artificial Intelligence Applications

Ali Soofastaei

"The key challenge is not so much globalization. It is what I call the fourth industrial revolution. Because its technology which creates major changes in our daily lives. It's a technology that creates fears. What we want to do is make the world much more aware. On the one hand of the opportunity of the new technology but on the other hand the risks and dangers we encounter".

—Klaus Schwab

1. Introduction

The opportunities and complexities associated with the digital era can be overwhelming to industries and markets, which face an enormous amount of potential information in each transaction. Being aware of trends in the data pool and benefiting from hidden information has created a new paradigm, redefining the meaning of corporate power. Access to information can make organizations more effective and help them to reach their goals. Big data analytics (BDA) enables industries to describe, diagnose, predict, prescribe, and find hidden growth opportunities, potentially increasing business value. BDA uses advanced analytical techniques to enhance knowledge and improve decision-making by reducing the complexity of exponentially increasing amounts of data. BDA uses novel and sophisticated algorithms to analyze real-time data, resulting in highly accurate analytics. Depending on the problem being solved, these complex algorithms can be allocated to either deep learning or machine learning (ML) approaches.

A significant consequence of the digital world is the creation of bulk raw data. Managers are responsible for managing this valuable capital, with its various shapes and sizes, on the basis of organizational needs. Big data has the power to affect all aspects of society, from social to educational. As the volume of raw data increases, particularly in technology-based companies, the issue of managing it becomes more critical. The variety, velocity, and volume of raw data warrant the use of advanced tools to overcome its complexity and to reveal the hidden information embedded in it. Thus, BDA has been proposed as a means of experimentation, simulation, data analysis, and monitoring. One BDA tool, advanced analytics (AA), can provide the foundation for predictive analysis on the basis of supervised and unsupervised data input. A reciprocal relationship exists between the power of AA and data input—the more precise and accurate the input data, the more effective the analytical performance. Additionally, ML, artificial intelligence (AI) and deep learning as subfields of AA can be used to extract knowledge from hidden data trends [1].

IntechOpen

The growing rate of data production in the digital era has introduced the concept of big data, which is defined by its significant volume, variety, veracity, velocity, and high value. Big data has created challenges for analysis, requiring organizations to deploy new analytical approaches and tools to overcome the complexity and magnitude of different data types (structured, semi-structured, and unstructured). Thus, BDA offers a sophisticated technique that can analyze an enormous volume of data and manage its complexity.

BDA can be used to support projects in innovation, productivity, and competition [2] by examining, processing, discovering, and exhibiting results to uncover hidden patterns and provide insights into interesting contextual relationships [3]. Complexity reduction and managing the cognitive burden of a knowledge-based society are key benefits of BDA. The most critical contributor to the success of BDA is feature identification, which defines the most crucial elements affecting results. This is followed by identifying correlations between inputs and a dynamic given point, which can change from time to time [3].

As a result of the rapid evolution of BDA, e-commerce and global connectivity have flourished. Governments have also taken advantage of BDA to provide improved services to their citizens [3]. Specific applications of BDA for the management and analysis of big data include business and social media. BDA can improve understanding of customer behaviors and handling of the five features of big data—volume, velocity, value, variety, and veracity. BDA not only provides businesses with a comprehensive view of consumer behavior but also enables organizations to be more innovative and effective in deploying strategies. Small- and medium-sized companies can use BDA to mine semi-structured big data, improving the quality of product recommendation systems and website design [4]. As suggested by [5], the use of BDA technology and techniques for large volumes of data can improve firm performance.

AA, AI, ML, predictive and prescriptive analytics, optimization models, decision-making algorithms, natural language processing, and robotic process automation have been popular keywords in various industrial studies in recent years. Industry managers and key decision-makers who are aware of the ability of AA to solve business problems are now competing for intelligent technologies and experts to operate them. However, investments in technology and data scientists do not guarantee success. Industrial managers must develop a strong foundation by embedding an understanding of AA within their companies. Three factors contribute to a thriving AA culture: people, strategy, and technology. The knowledge of individuals in companies plays a critical role in the success of the analytics revolution because there are no practical solutions for applying AA when a company is faced with unacceptable levels of knowledge and experience. Management strategies can be implemented to ensure that project teams are sufficiently flexible to adapt to solutions to work processes suggested by the AA. The level of technology is also essential for the accuracy of analytics and can be a critical parameter when the outcomes of AA are used to improve business processes.

AA and AI, defined as intelligence demonstrated by machines, have many applications. AA has been applied in many fields and industries, including agriculture [6, 7], oil and gas [8], aviation [9–15], computer science [16], deepfake [17, 18], education [19–21], finance [22], government, heavy industry, history [23], telecommunication maintenance, toys and games [24], hospitals and medicine [25–27], recruiting, human resources and job search engines [28, 29], military [30, 31], news services [32, 33], writing and publishing, online conference services [34–36], power electronics [37], sensors [38], and transport [39, 40].

DOI: http://dx.doi.org/10.5772/intechopen.89784

2. Artificial intelligence: applications and challenges

AI capabilities are rapidly evolving, and it is essential to build a framework to model the AI application process from study to implementation. **Figure 1** illustrates the general application of AI.

The critical challenge for using AI in industrial projects is to demonstrate the value of processed data in making intelligent predictions and optimizing decision-making. Overall, there are four significant challenges for the employment of AI in different industries: data, speed, high reliability, and interpretability.

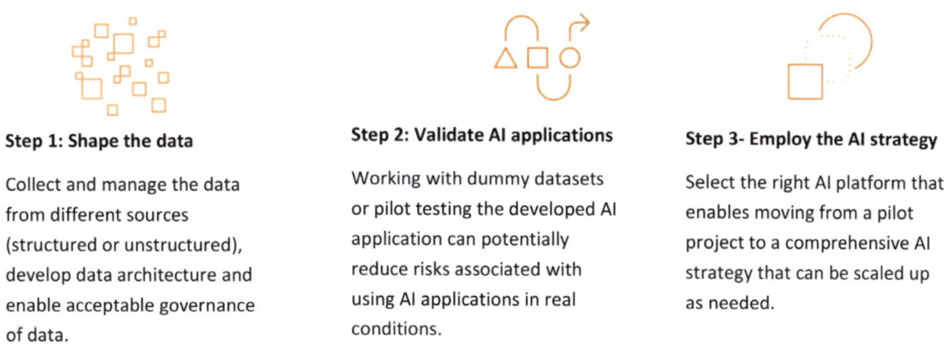

Figure 1.
Steps in applying artificial intelligence (AI).

2.1 Data

Industrial systems produce large volumes of data, and advanced engineering is undoubtedly a big data environment. Collected data are typically structured. However, when faced with a low-quality dataset, industrial operations can generate data with "3B" (**b**ad, **b**roken, and illogical **b**ackground) issues. 3B issues can potentially create challenges in implementing ML and AI solutions for solving business problems. In some industries, the quality of data is insufficient to train and validate sophisticated algorithms such as deep learning models. This problem has been a major challenge for data scientists and data analysis in the development of prediction and optimization applications.

Moreover, real collected data from sites cannot cover all requirements and there are many gaps in datasets. A lack of data can be a crucial problem when data scientists are seeking comprehensive datasets to cover all working conditions. Further, AI solutions should be generated based on reliable historical information; however, in many cases, there is a lack of available data to make sustainable models.

2.2 Speed

With the evolution of technology across various industries, operational processes can rapidly produce large amounts of information. The use of intelligent applications is essential for working with enormous amounts of generated real-time data to reduce resource waste and operational risk. Nowadays, key industries use cloud-based approaches not only to store data but also to improve ease of access to information. However, these approaches still fail to meet the specific requirements for calculation effectiveness.

2.3 High reliability

AI solutions are strongly related to background processes and collected datasets. In other words, the reliability of AI applications depends on the quality of historical information. AA applications usually deal with critical challenges related to security, maintenance, operations, energy consumption, and safety. Dissatisfaction with prediction, optimization, or decision-making algorithms may lead to negative outcomes and discourage users from relying on AA approaches such as AI systems.

2.4 Interpretability

AI can help improve the accuracy and reliability of prediction and optimization of industrial applications. However, interpreting the results is a significant challenge for experts and managers when using AI to solve business problems. A practical solution for industry may be to train experts, specialists, and managers to operate the analytics and provide root cause analysis for anomalies. This implies that during the development of applications, data scientists should work with experts and managers to include domain knowledge in algorithm expansion processes and ensure that models can adaptively learn and accumulate knowledge.

3. Predictive models

Predictive modeling is the term used for the process of utilizing data mining and probability to forecast future outcomes. A predictive (forecasting) model uses several independent variables or predictors that are likely to influence the desired dependent variable (forecasting output). Once data have been collected for the relevant predictors, a statistical algorithm is deployed. This algorithm may be a simple linear equation or a sophisticated ML algorithm such as a neural network. Predictive modeling mainly overlaps with the field of ML, and many of the algorithms utilized in forecasting models are found in the context of ML and AI.

Predictive modeling is often associated with weather forecasting, online advertising, and marketing. However, it also has applications in mining engineering.

One of the most frequently overlooked challenges of the forecasting model is obtaining suitable data to apply when creating algorithms. Data collection and preparation is the most challenging step in developing a predictive model, and it is essential to locate the best predictors to feed into the model. A descriptive analysis of the data and data treatment, including missing values and outlier fixing, is a crucial task that consumes most of the time needed in predictive modeling.

Once the data have been collected, the next step is to select an appropriate model. Linear regressions are among the most accessible models for predictive algorithms, but other multifaceted AI models are available. The complexity of the model does not guarantee the performance of the prediction. Model selection should be considered in relation to data availability and quality and the forecasting period.

After modeling, a production estimation should be provided to measure the accuracy of the model.

Some well-known predictive modeling methods widely used in industrial applications are regression, time series algorithms, deep learning, and ML.

4. Optimization methods

Many different practical optimization methods have been used in critical industries. Generally, the aim of optimization is to increase productivity, energy and cost efficiency, and safety. Prior to the data revolution, traditional optimization models were used for practical business solutions. Currently, the quantity and quality of collected data in many industries have created an opportunity to use innovative optimization solutions to achieve better outcomes. Of all the current optimization approaches, genetic algorithm, particle swarm, ant colony, bee colony, firefly algorithm (FA), and tabu search are the most prevalent in critical industries.

The aforementioned AA, BDA, and AI applications for prediction, optimization, and decision-making may help industries increase efficiency across various dimensions as well as take action to solve global environmental and energy consumption problems. The case studies presented in the following chapters illustrate the possibilities for using AA, BDA, and AI to solve business problems across different industries.

Author details

Ali Soofastaei
Artificial Intelligence Center, Vale, Brisbane, Australia

*Address all correspondence to: ali@soofastaei.net

References

[1] Jan B et al. Deep learning in big data analytics: A comparative study. Computers and Electrical Engineering. 2017;**2**(3):542-551

[2] Esposito C et al. A knowledge-based platform for Big Data analytics based on publish/subscribe services and stream processing. Knowledge-Based Systems. 2015;**79**:3-17

[3] Iqbal R et al. Big data analytics: Computational intelligence techniques and application areas. Technological Forecasting and Social Change. 2018;**1**(2):416-427

[4] Gandomi A, Haider M. Beyond the hype: Big data concepts, methods, and analytics. International Journal of Information Management. 2015;**35**(2):137-144

[5] Chen J-L. The synergistic effects of IT-enabled resources on organizational capabilities and firm performance. Information & Management. 2012;**49**(3-4):142-150

[6] Intel. The Future of AI in Agriculture. 2019. Available from: https://www.intel.com/content/www/us/en/big-data/article/agriculture-harvests-big-data.html

[7] Sennaar K. AI in Agriculture—Present Applications and Impact. 2019. Available from: https://emerj.com/ai-sector-overviews/ai-agriculture-present-applications-impact/

[8] Aminzadeh F. Applications of AI and soft computing for challenging problems in the oil industry. Journal of Petroleum Science and Engineering. 2005;**47**(1-2):5-14

[9] Gallagher S. AI bests Air Force combat tactics experts in simulated dogfights. ARC Technica. 2016;**2**(1):94-107

[10] Jones RM et al. Automated intelligent pilots for combat flight simulation. AI Magazine. 1999;**20**(1):22-27

[11] Group KBS. AIDA: Artificial Intelligence Supported Design of Aircraft. 2017. Available from: www.kbs.twi.tudelft.nl

[12] Tomayko JE. The Story of Self-Repairing Flight Control Systems. 2018. Available from: https://crgis.ndc.nasa.gov/crgis/images/c/c9/88798main_srfcs.pdf

[13] Schweikhard KA. Flight demonstration of X-33 vehicle health management system components on the F/A-18 systems research aircraft. Technical Information Service Journal. 2008;**6**(1):5-15

[14] Adams E. AI Wields the Power to Make Flying Safer—And Maybe Even Pleasant. 2017. Available from: https://www.wired.com/2017/03/ai-wields-power-make-flying-safer-maybe-even-pleasant/

[15] Haitham Baomar PJB. An intelligent autopilot system that learns flight emergency procedures by imitating human pilots. IEEE Symposium Series on Computational Intelligence. 2016;**1**(1):1-9

[16] Independent T. Google AI Creates its Own "Child Bot". 2017. Available from: https://www.independent.co.uk/life-style/gadgets-and-tech/news/google-child-ai-bot-nasnet-automl-machine-learning-artificial-intelligence-a8093201.html

[17] Nießner M. Face2Face: Real-Time Face Capture and Reenactment of RGB Videos. 2019. Available from: http://www.niessnerlab.org/projects/thies2016face.html

[18] Will 'Deepfakes' Disrupt the Midterm Election? 2019. Available

from: https://www.wired.com/story/will-deepfakes-disrupt-the-midterm-election/?verso=true

[19] Sears A. The Role of Artificial Intelligence in the Classroom. 2018. Available from: https://elearningindustry.com/artificial-intelligence-in-the-classroom-role

[20] Quan-Haase A. Technology and society: Social networks, power, and inequality. Oxford University. 2016;**2**(1):43-44

[21] Richtel M. Growing up Digital, Wired for Distraction. 2010. Available from: https://www.nytimes.com/2010/11/21/technology/21brain.html?pagewanted=1&_r=3

[22] Chen J. Algorithmic trading. Investopedia. 2019;**2**(1):45-58

[23] Robotics IIFO. World Robotics 2015 Industrial Robots. 2019. Available from: https://web.archive.org/web/20160327031517/http://www.ifr.org/industrial-robots/statistics/

[24] Lennihan M. How Artificial Intelligence Is Moving from the Lab to your Kid's Playroom. 2016. Available from: https://www.washingtonpost.com/news/innovations/wp/2015/10/15/how-artificial-intelligence-is-moving-from-the-lab-to-your-kids-playroom/?noredirect=on

[25] Reed TRR, Nancy E, Fritzson P. Heart sound analysis for symptom detection and computer-aided diagnosis. Simulation Modelling Practice and Theory. 2004;**12**(2):129-146

[26] Yorita AK, Naoyuki. Cognitive development in partner robots for information support to elderly people. IEEE Transactions on Autonomous Mental Development. 2011;**3**(1):64-73

[27] Luxton DD. Artificial intelligence in psychological practice: Current and future applications and implications. Professional Psychology: Research and Practice. 2014;**45**(5):332-339

[28] Strauss K. The Role of Artificial Intelligence in the Future of Job Search. 2018. Available from: https://www.forbes.com/sites/karstenstrauss/2018/02/02/the-role-of-artificial-intelligence-in-the-future-of-job-search/#2bf33fad4cb0

[29] Chamberlain A. What's Ahead for Jobs? Five Disruptions to Watch in 2018. 2017. Available from: https://www.glassdoor.com/research/app/uploads/sites/2/2017/12/Final_GD_ResearchReport_5Disruptions2018.pdf

[30] Requena G et al. Melomics music medicine (M3) to lessen pain perception during pediatric prick test procedure. Pediatric Allergy and Immunology. 2014;**25**(7):721-724

[31] Souppouris A. Google's 'Magenta' Project Will See if AIs Can Truly Make Art. 2019. Available from: https://www.engadget.com/2016/05/23/google-magenta-machine-learning-music-art/

[32] Meehan JR. Tale-spin, an interactive program that writes stories. In: Proceedings of the 5th International Joint Conference on Artificial Intelligence; Vol. 1, Issue 2; 1977. pp. 91-98

[33] Olewitz C. A Japanese A.I. Program Just Wrote a Short Novel, and it Almost Won a Literary Prize. 2016. Available from: https://www.digitaltrends.com/cool-tech/japanese-ai-writes-novel-passes-first-round-nationanl-literary-prize/

[34] Kongthon A et al. Implementing an online help desk system based on conversational agent. In: Proceedings of the International Conference on Management of Emergent Digital

EcoSystems Article No. 69; Vol. 1, Issue 1; 2009. pp. 450-454

[35] O'Brien SA. Is this App the Call Center of the Future? 2016. Available from: https://money.cnn.com/2016/01/12/technology/startup-pypestream/

[36] Clark J. New Google AI Brings Automation to Customer Service. 2016. Available from: https://www.bloomberg.com/news/articles/2016-07-20/new-google-ai-services-bring-automation-to-customer-service-iqv2rshg

[37] Dragičević T, Wheeler P, Blaabjerg F. Artificial intelligence aided automated design for reliability of power electronic systems. IEEE Transactions on Power Electronics. 2019;**34**(8):7161-7171

[38] Ideacuria Inc. AI Sensor Technology. 2019. Available from: https://www.ideacuria.com/ic/aisensor_technology.html

[39] Johns RC. Artificial Intelligence in Transportation Information for Application. 2007. Available from: http://onlinepubs.trb.org/onlinepubs/circulars/ec113.pdf

[40] Hallerbach S et al. Simulation-based identification of critical scenarios for cooperative and automated vehicles. SAE International. 2018;**1**(2):93-106

Chapter 2

Bio-Inspired Hybrid Algorithm for Web Services Clustering

Maricela Bravo, Román A. Mora-Gutiérrez and Luis F. Hoyos-Reyes

Abstract

Web services clustering is the task of extracting and selecting the features from a collection of Web services and forming groups of closely related services. The implementation of novel and efficient algorithms for Web services clustering is relevant for the organization of service repositories on the Web. Counting with well-organized collections of Web services promotes the efficiency of Web service discovery, search, selection, substitution, and invocation. In recent years, methods inspired by nature using biological analogies have been adapted for clustering problems, among which genetic algorithms, evolutionary strategies, and algorithms that imitate the behavior of some animal species have been implemented. Computation inspired by nature aims at imitating the steps that nature has developed and adapting them to find a solution of a given problem. In this chapter, we investigate how biologically inspired clustering methods can be applied to clustering Web services and present a hybrid approach for Web services clustering using the Artificial Bee Colony (ABC) algorithm, K-means, and Consensus. This hybrid algorithm was implemented, and a series of experiments were conducted using three collections of Web services. Results of the experiments show that the solution approach is adequate and efficient to carry out the clustering of very large collections of Web services.

Keywords: artificial bee colony, K-means, Consensus, hybrid algorithms, Web services clustering, semantic similarity measures

1. Introduction

Web services clustering is the task of selecting and extracting the features of a collection of Web services, discovering the similarities between them to form groups or classes considering those features. The implementation of novel and efficient algorithms for the automatic clustering of Web services is relevant for the organization of large collections of services in private or public network such as the Internet. Having a directory of Web services organized in groups according to one or more characteristics represents an advantage during the search, selection, invocation, substitution, and composition of Web services.

Methods inspired by nature using biological analogies have been adapted for clustering problems, among which genetic algorithms, evolutionary strategies, and algorithms that imitate the behavior of some animal species have been implemented. Living beings such as animals and plants and even the climate exhibit extraordinary, complex, and fascinating natural phenomena. Of particular interest is the intelligent behavior of some animal species to find a solution to solve a problem and maintain the perfect balance of the environment surrounding.

This is the main idea of computation inspired by nature, that is, to imitate the steps that nature has developed and adapt them to find a solution of a problem, thus converting it into a bio-inspired algorithm. This is the main reason for the implementation of an algorithm that exploits the collective intelligence of a Bee Colony as an alternative for clustering. This chapter presents an innovative approach for Web services clustering using a hybrid algorithm based on the Artificial Bee Colony, K-means, and Consensus.

The work described in this chapter is part of a research project whose objective is to design and implement a semantic directory of Web services using efficient, fully automated methods to allow the organization, composition, and classification of Web services with a semantic approach.

Figure 1 shows the general architecture of the semantic directory and a methodology to construct and manage the directory. The methodology consists of the following phases:

1. *Public Web service retrieval* aims at searching over the Internet to find and copy Web service descriptions (files formatted in WSDL description language) in a local file directory. Web service retrieval is executed through crawlers designed specifically to parse and identify links to files in WSDL.

2. *Extraction and analysis of Web services* consists of parsing every Web service description file and the extraction of specific data, such as: method names, input and output parameters, and port types to facilitate the automatic invocation. Extracted data is stored in an ontology model. For this phase, we use a tool which transforms WSDL files into an ontological representation.

3. *Web service similarity calculation* is an important phase of the methodology, because classification and clustering of Web services requires the calculation of distances between services. In order to calculate similarities, different measures can be implemented and combined to obtain better results.

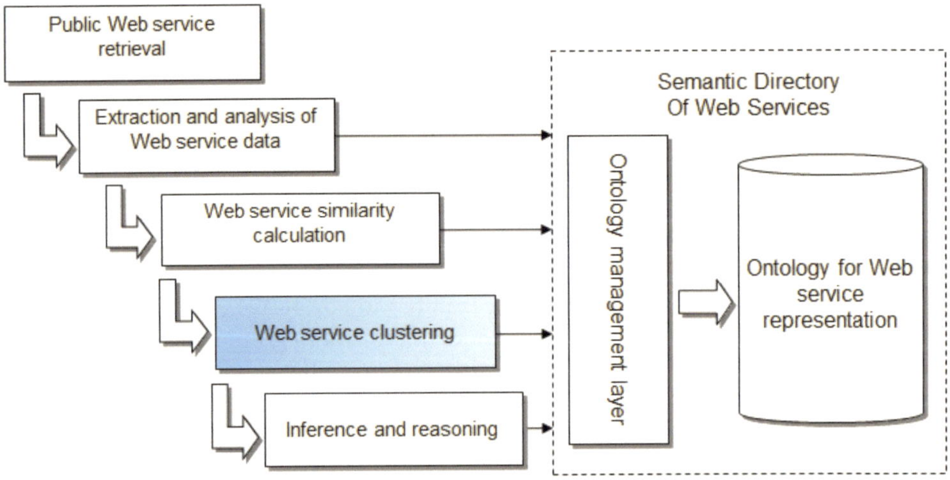

Figure 1.
Semantic directory of Web services.

4. *Web service classification and clustering* consists of selecting and extracting the characteristics of a collection of Web services and discovering the similarities between them to form groups or classes considering those characteristics. Therefore, this phase depends on the results of the previous phases. In particular, in this chapter a hybrid clustering algorithm based on the Artificial Bee Colony algorithm, the K-means, and Consensus is described.

5. *Inference and reasoning* represents the supporting mechanisms to exploit and utilize the enriched Web service ontologies.

2. Related work

Web service classification and clustering is a topic addressed form different perspectives such as statistical, stochastic, and novel approaches based on bio-inspired algorithms. Additionally, semantic approaches to describe, discover, and invoke Web services have been studied to propose novel clustering algorithms. In this section a revision of related work is presented considering two trends: reported work that address clustering and classification of Web services and clustering approaches based on bio-inspired algorithms. **Table 1** presents the main characteristics of related work.

In 2009, Liang et al. [1] proposed a method for Web service categorization considering keywords and semantic relations between elements of the description. Their proposed methodology involves preprocessing WSDL documents, rough clustering by labeling Web services with class tag, and fine clustering.

In 2009, Platzer et al. [2] described a scalable approach for clustering very large service repositories. They use a statistical clustering algorithm enhancing a vector space to support the search of services related to a given query.

In 2012, Pop et al. [3] presented two approaches for service clustering, one inspired by the behavior of the birds and other inspired by the behavior of ants. They implemented methods to evaluate the semantic similarity between services.

In 2013, Du et al. [4] presented an approach for clustering Web services based on functional similarity and refinement of clusters using a concept position vector.

In 2014, Wu et al. [5] presented an approach which consists of three modules: data preprocessing, Web service tag recommendation, and Web services clustering. The first module consists of building a content vector formed with nouns, verbs, or adjectives. Authors use different features and different approaches for similarity computation. For content use the normalized Google distance, for data types and messages they use a basic match similarity, and for tag similarity they apply the Jaccard coefficient.

In 2014, Prakash and Singh [6] compared the performance of evolutionary algorithms: Genetic Algorithm, Differential Evolution, Particle Swarm Optimization, and Artificial Bee Colony for clustering three real and one synthetic data sets.

In 2017, Sahoo [7] presented a two-step ABC algorithm for data clustering problems. Authors addressed the three problems of the ABC algorithm such as initial positions of food sources, solution search equation, and abandoned food location.

In 2018, Kotekar and Kamath [8] described a Web services clustering approach based on Cat Swarm Optimization (CSO), which emulates the social behavior of cats in nature.

Automated Web services clustering is useful to facilitate service search, service discovery, service composition, and service substitution. Of particular interest is the representation of Web services through ontologies because the purpose of this work is the automatic organization of any collection (public or private) of Web service in ontologies and their semantic enrichment by classification and clustering.

Work	Input data	Clustering approach	Use of ontologies	Similarity approach	Number of Web services used	Service repository	Benefits	Limitations
Liang et al. [1]	WSDL documents	Incremental K-means algorithm Bisecting K-means	No	Tree-based structure matching	352	Xmethods.com Bindingpoint.com Webservicelist.com Xignite.com	This approach clusters Web service documents	The similarity approach is not semantic, and the clustering method is not bio-inspired
Platzer et al. [2]	WSDL documents	Statistical clustering analysis	No	Euclidean distance	275	Xmethods.com	This approach clusters Web service documents	The clustering method is not based on novel bio-inspired algorithms. Similarity measure is not semantic
Pop et al. [3]	WSDL documents extracted from OWL-TC4	Particle swarm and ant-based service clustering	Yes	Semantic similarity by evaluating the Degree of Match (DoM)	894	SAWSDL-TC collection	The solution approach is very similar to the approach described in this chapter. The main difference is on the algorithms utilized	The semantic similarity does not use a lexical database to improve similarity measures
Du et al. [4]	WSDL documents extracted from OWL-TC4	Bottom-up hierarchical clustering	No	Semantic similarity based on WordNet	1075	OWL-TC4 collection	This work is closely related with the approach presented in this chapter	The clustering method is not based on novel bio-inspired algorithms
Wu et al. [5]	WSDL documents	K-means	No	The similarity integrates all the feature measures using a weighed sum	15,968	Seekda	This approach clusters Web service documents	The clustering method is not based on bio-inspired algorithms. Similarity measure is not semantic
Prakash and	Data is based on three real and	Genetic Algorithm, Differential Evolution, Particle Swarm	No	Not specified	Not for Web services	No	The clustering approach is based on novel bio-inspired algorithms.	The clustering method is not applied to Web services

DOI: http://dx.doi.org/10.5772/intechopen.85200

Work	Input data	Clustering approach	Use of ontologies	Similarity approach	Number of Web services used	Service repository	Benefits	Limitations
Singh [6]	one synthetic data sets	Optimization and Artificial Bee Colony						
Sahoo [7]	Data is downloaded from UCI repository	Two-step ABC algorithm	No	Euclidean distance	Not for Web services	Data sets are downloaded from the UCI repository	The clustering approach is based on novel bio-inspired algorithms	The clustering method is not applied to Web services. Similarity measure is not semantic
Kotekar and Kamath [8]	WSDL documents extracted from OWL-TC4	Cat Swarm Optimization (CSO)	No	Euclidean distance and TF-IDF	1083	OWL-TC4 collection	The clustering approach is based on novel bio-inspired algorithms	Similarity measure is not semantic

Table 1.
Comparison of related work.

3. Clustering process

Clustering of Web services consist of partitioning the set of Web services in the collection into an appropriate number of clusters based on a similarity measure. Therefore, services in the same cluster are more similar than the services in the different clusters [6].

In this section the clustering approach implemented is described. This process has as input a collection of Web services formatted according to Web Service Description Language (WSDL). This collection of Web services is processed utilizing specific parsers to extract the most important data of the service description, which are the method names and input and output parameters. The detailed process is described in the following subsections (**Figure 2**).

3.1 Extracting and parsing

Every Web service description includes the definition of the programming interfaces to be invoked remotely. **Figure 3** shows the abstract service interface

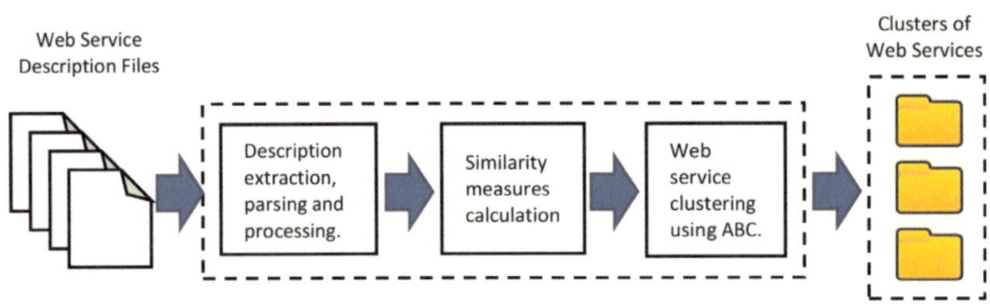

Figure 2.
Clustering process of Web services.

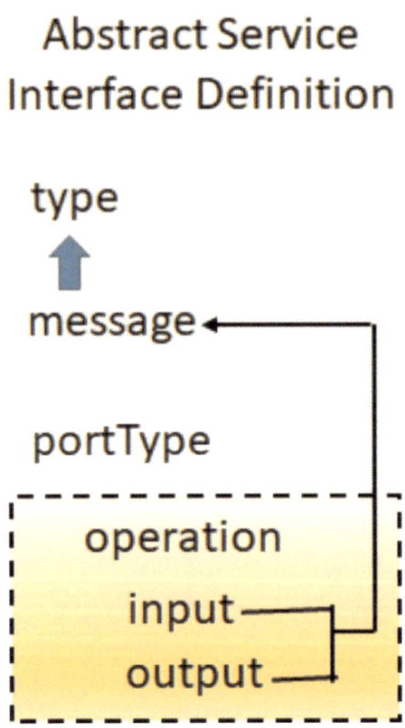

Figure 3.
Web service interface definition.

Semantic similarity measure	Description	Approach	Advantage
Lesk [10]; Banerjee and Pedersen [11]	Address word sense disambiguation by counting overlaps between dictionary definitions	Corpus-based approach	It is not a syntactic technique, and it is not dependent on global information
Wu and Palmer [12]	Path length to the root node from the least common super-concept of two concepts	Taxonomic-based approach	It is a syntactic-semantic technique
Resnik [13]	Evaluate the semantic similarity in a taxonomy, based on the notion of information content	It is a hybrid approach that combines corpus-based statistical methods with knowledge-based taxonomic information	It is a semantic technique
Jian and Conrath [14]	It combines a lexical taxonomy structure with corpus statistical information	It is a hybrid approach that combines taxonomic-based approach with corpus-based approach	Based on the tests reported, this combined approach outperforms other computational models
Lin [15]	This measure uses the amount of information needed to state the commonality between the two concepts and the information needed to describe these terms	Information content measure (corpus-based)	It is a universally applicable similarity measure, independent of domain or form of knowledge representation
Hirst Onge [16]	This measure states that two lexicalized concepts are semantically close if their synonyms are connected by a path that is not too long, and it is not changing its direction frequently	Information content measure that uses lexical chains as a context	It is a semantic and context-based technique
Leacock and Chodorow [17]	This measure finds the shortest path length between two concepts, and scales that value by the maximum path length in the is-A hierarchy in which they occur	This is an information content measure that adds topical to local context using a statistical classifier	It is a semantic and context-based technique

Table 2.
Summary of similarity measurements.

definition; from this, the elements extracted for similarity calculation are the name of the operations and their associated input and output parameters.

4. Semantic similarity measures

Measuring the similarity between two concepts is not a new topic. Throughout the last decades, many measures of similarity have been reported using different perspectives: syntactic, semantic, contextual, etc. In this work, we use a set of semantic similarity measurements based on WordNet.[1] Computing similarity

[1]https://wordnet.princeton.edu/

between all Web services in the collection is a process executed in pairs. Let *W* be the tuple that represents all Web services in the collection as follows:

$$\mathrm{W} = \langle \mathrm{P}, \mathrm{I}, \mathrm{O} \rangle \tag{1}$$

where *P*, represents all operation names; *I*, is the set of input parameters; *O*, is the set of output parameters.

In particular, in this work the similarity measures were applied only on the operation names. Therefore, the similarity calculation takes as input a matrix of all operation names in the collection of Web services, that is, as follows:

$$(\text{Let})\ P = \{p_1, p_2, p_3, \dots, p_n\} \tag{2}$$

$$\text{Input Matrix} = \left\{ \left(\mathrm{p_{i,}}\, \mathrm{q_i} \right) \in \mathrm{P} \times \mathrm{P}, 1 \leq \mathrm{i} \leq \mathrm{n} \right\} \tag{3}$$

Eight measures that exploit WordNet database were used to calculate the semantic similarity between Web service operations. WordNet is a lexical database available online; it is organized into five categories: nouns, verbs, adjectives, adverbs, and function words [9]. The utilization of WordNet for semantic similarity measurements is a good approach in contrast with the traditional syntactic similarity approaches, specifically in the case of service operations, as they normally include a verb indicating the main functionality of the operation method.

Additionally, an application programming interface (API) that implements a large collection of semantic similarity measures (140 methods) is available WNetSSAPI[2]. A deeper analysis and comparison of similarity measures is out of the scope of this work. **Table 2** shows a summary of the semantic similarity measures used.

With these measures, all service operations are compared, and a set of eight matrixes are created with the distances between them. **Figure 4** shows an example of the calculation of the eight similarities with operation names.

```
SimilarityBetween( ChangeAngleUnit , ChangeAreaUnit ) =
==> Jacquard Syntactic Similarity = 0.5
==> Wu Palmer Semantic Similarity = 0.5994745994745996
==> Lin Semantic Similarity = 0.4535231912829227
==> Path Semantic Similarity = 0.33355780022446685
==> Lesk Semantic Similarity = 0.6666666666666666
==> HirstStOnge Semantic Similarity = 1.0
==> JiangConrath Semantic Similarity = 0.2985112762922702
==> LeacockChodorow Semantic Similarity = 0.8320633585750906
==> Resnik Semantic Similarity = 0.5883605316331607
```

Figure 4.
Example of the calculation of semantic similarities.

[2]http://wnetss-api.smr-team.org/

5. Artificial Bee Colony algorithm

The Artificial Bee Colony (ABC) algorithm is an optimization technique that simulates the foraging behavior of honey bees and has been successfully applied to various practical problems and is a nature-inspired and swarm intelligence method that has been applied in different scenarios with good results. The ABC algorithm was proposed in 2005 by Karaboga [18, 19]; accordingly, the collective intelligence model of the Bee Colony consists of:

a. *Employed foragers* which are bees assigned (employed) to a particular food source and are exploiting it. They carry information about the food source, distance and direction to the nest and the profitability of the source, and are capable of sharing this information.

b. *Unemployed foragers* are bees that are continuously searching for food sources. These unemployed bees are subdivided into *scouts*, bees that search on the surrounding environment for new food sources, and *onlookers*, bees that wait in the nest.

The ABC algorithm has different modes of behavior:

a. Exploration is the task executed by unemployed bees to find new food sources.

b. Exploitation is the task executed by employed bees on a food source.

c. Recruitment is the action that an unemployed bee executes with forager bees to exploit a food source.

d. Abandonment of a nectar source occurs when a better food source is found.

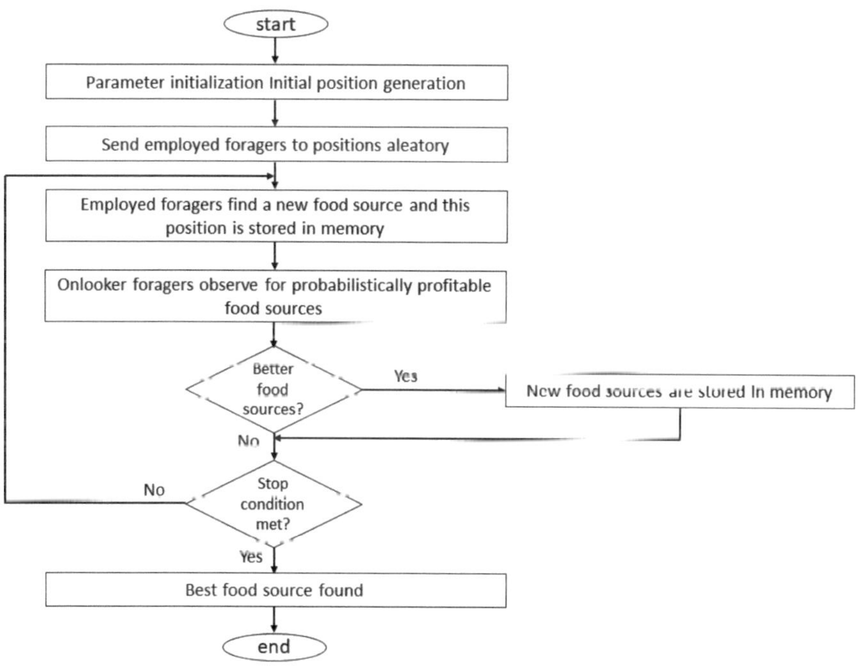

Figure 5.
ABC algorithm general workflow.

An important behavior of *employed* and *onlooker* bees is their capacity of sharing information (memory) to choose and adjust the food source value. This value depends on the proximity to the nest, the richness or concentration of honey energy [18]. The exchange of information occurs during the waggle dance at the hive. *Onlooker* foragers watch numerous dances at the dancing area and decide to employ themselves at the most profitable food source. When an *onlooker* forager recruit starts searching and locates the food source, then it utilizes its own capability to memorize the location and starts exploiting it. The *onlooker* forager becomes an *employed* forager. In the ABC algorithm the set of possible solutions represent the food sources, and the food source value represents the quality of the solution. A general representation of the ABC workflow algorithm is presented in **Figure 5**.

6. Hybrid algorithm description

A hybrid algorithm was proposed to make the ABC auto-adjustable during each iteration to decide the number of clusters by incorporating K-means and a Consensus method. In particular, K-means is used to select the elements inside each generated cluster to decide centroids for similarity calculations. The solution of the algorithm is represented as a vector of size n (number of Web services to cluster) where each position of the element in the vector is the group to which it belongs to.

6.1 Objective function

The objective function of this hybrid algorithm is shown in Eq. (4):

$$\text{Min} \sum_{\substack{i=1 \\ x \in c_i \\ y \in c_i}}^{C} d(x_i, y_i) \tag{4}$$

where d, distance between centroid of cluster y_i and a service x_i; y_i, centroid of cluster i; x_i: one of the services included in cluster i. No group of services should be empty, and there should be no intersection between groups.

6.2 Filtering similarities

The first stage of the hybrid algorithm consists of filtering of the eight matrices that contain the information of similarities between Web services. The filtering consists of discarding values that exceed the limits allowed and established by the similarity measures, as a result of this filtering, new matrices are generated with a degree of 95% certainty in the measurements. Eq. (5) shows the filtering calculation:

$$X - 1.96 \frac{\sigma}{\sqrt{N}} \leq \mu \leq X + 1.96 \frac{\sigma}{\sqrt{N}} \tag{5}$$

where X, average matrix; 1.96, table value; σ, standard deviation; N, element of the similarity matrix; μ, average similarity.

6.3 Food source representation

After the filtering process, all obtained data is stored in an average matrix (food sources) discarding the positions that contain null or zero information; that is, the average matrix was calculated considering only those values that were filtered and accepted as feasible values that contribute with information to the hybrid algorithm.

6.4 Bee's representation

Using the average matrix a set of arrays is generated representing the bees and other important information as the number of groups and centroids. **Table 3** shows the structure of the solution generated.

a. *Max group*. This hybrid algorithm does not require the user to indicate how many groups it should generate; the algorithm as it iterates determines how many groups to generate based on the results obtained on the previous iteration and applying the Consensus method. Initially, the *i-th* bee will generate a random number of groups, based on a discrete uniform distribution with limits 2 to N/2; in the subsequent iterations of the algorithm, the *i-th* bee will produce a random number γ (based on a normal distribution of the weighted variance of the Max group determined by the colony in the previous iteration), then a simple rounding will be applied to γ.

b. *Centroids*. Next, the *i-th* bee must determine the centroids of the γ groups involved in the classification. The centroid sub-vector is formed by N integer elements, where x_{ijk} is zero if it is not considered as a centroid for any group, in case $x_{ijk} = u$ implies that the *j-th* Web service is centroid of the *k-th* group. Initially such values are assigned randomly; later by applying Eq. (6), the values of the sub-vector are obtained:

$$X'_{new} = \text{round}\left(X'_i - \phi(X'_i - X'_s)\right) \tag{6}$$

where X'_{new}, new vector; X'_i, first vector generated by the algorithm; ϕ, aleatory number between 0 and 1

a. $\boldsymbol{\beta}$ represents the sum of the similarity between centroids of the groups, while $\boldsymbol{\alpha}$ is the summation of the similarity between members of each group to the corresponding centroid. The objective is to minimize $\boldsymbol{\beta}$ and maximize $\boldsymbol{\alpha}$ simultaneously.

b. For each bee the *assessment* function is calculated using $f(x) = \frac{1}{\beta} + \alpha$; the objective is to obtain the highest $f(x)$ value. During each iteration, the $f(x)$ value is stored in the solution vector.

c. Normalization is used to determine the quality of the food source found. Normalization is calculated with $n_i = \frac{f(x_i)}{\sum_{i=1}^{N} f(x_i)}$. The bee will abandon the food source if there is a better food source in the near surrounding.

Groups generated	Centroids	β	α	Normalization	Assessment	Max group	Limit
32,231	32,001	1.068	1.55	0.301	0.36	3	5

Table 3.
Composition of the vector with information of generated groups.

Input: Number of bees (B), Filtered similarity matrix, Number of Web services to cluster (M), number of maximum iterations (v), value of φ

Output: Best classification found by the ABC algorithm

For each of the N food sources execute algorithm of Fig. 7
Calculate normalization value
v'=0
While v'≤v
    Compute mean ($\bar{c}$) and variance (S_c) weighed (base on normalization values) of groups used by employed bees at iteration v'-1.
    For each bee
        Search for food source at neighborhood of *i* using algorithm of Fig. 8
        If value of $f(x_{new})$ is better than f(x)
            Move employed bee to the new food source
            $limit_i$=0
        Else
            $limit_i$= $limit_i$+1;
        End If
        If ($limit_i$ = g)
            Aleatory generate a new food source
            Move the i-th bee to new food source
        End If
    End For
End While
Select bee with best *f*(*x*)

Figure 6.
ABC algorithm pseudocode.

Randomly determine the number of groups to generate (a uniform distributed value between 2 and *M*/2)
Randomly determine the centroids of each group. (Construction of the centroid vector)
Classify each of the *M* Web services in one of the groups according to the similarity to the centroids (application of the classic *k-means* algorithm)
Determine the corresponding assessment value.

Figure 7.
Pseudocode of the "Generation of N *initial food sources."*

d. Limit is a *counter* that indicates the number of iterations that the employed bee has being exploiting the current food source. The employed bee is obligated to abandon the food source when a *g* number of iterations is achieved (**Figures 6–8**).

Let a be an aleatory number with normal distribution, mean ($\bar{c}$) and variance (S_c)
The number of groups of the *i-th* bee is the rounded value of a that is within the limits
i' is a food source different from *i*, which is randomly selected based on the value of normalization.
With the centroid sub-vectors of *i* and *i'*
Generate x_{new}, which is a combination of centroid sub-vectors of *i* and *i'* using Equation (2)
Repair x_{new} in such a way that it contains exactly a cells different to zero, each with a different value between *i* and a.
For each of the m Web services
    Determine the similarity to the centroids of the *j-th* service.
    Assign the *j-th* service to the group with the highest similarity.
End For
Calculate β α and $f(x_{new})$

Figure 8.
Pseudocode of "Search for a food source in the neighborhood of i."

7. Experimentation and results

Experiments were carried out with three service collections, which involved grouping 50, 647, and 1027 Web services, respectively. For the creation of the similarity matrices, eight different semantic similarity measures were calculated for each collection of Web services. The resulting similarity matrices were filtered to discard values that exceed the allowed limits.

The determination of the parameters used by the algorithm was performed by brute force, resulting in using 10 and the value of "phi" (φ) set to 0.8; the value of the limit that makes up each vector from the beginning was established with the value of 10.

In order to characterize the behavior of the algorithm, 20 executions were made with 100, 200, and 500 iterations of the algorithm. For each of the executions, the best value of $f(x)$ found by the bees was determined. Subsequently, a statistical analysis of the results found was carried out. **Table 4** shows the average values of $f(x)$ for each of the instances with 100, 200, and 500 iterations, respectively.

Based on the results shown in **Table 4**, it can be affirmed that for the 50 services instance, the best values are found with 500 iterations, while for the instance of 647 services, the best values are obtained with 100 iterations. Finally, for the instance of 1027, it is obtained with 200 iterations.

Matrix size	100 iterations	200 iterations	500 iterations
	$f(x)$	$f(x)$	$f(x)$
50	0.4631	0.5011	0.5169
647	0.4457	0.4152	0.4228
1027	0.4414	0.4782	0.4542

Table 4.
Average results of collections executing 100, 200, and 500 iterations.

Collection-iterations	Best	Worst	Mean	Variance	Deviation
50–100	0.58936208	0.29274988	0.45901481	0.00593354	0.0770295
50–200	0.54853117	0.44904535	0.50052478	0.00088301	0.02971549
50–500	0.57163535	0.46554965	0.51820976	0.00090081	0.03001343
647–100	0.54947584	0.2153186	0.44401451	0.01027133	0.10134758
647–200	0.54778745	0.20257995	0.40923046	0.01554565	0.12468218
647–500	0.54881541	0.22262872	0.41911288	0.01280278	0.11314939
1027–100	0.55531806	0.27378002	0.44488931	0.00847871	0.09207991
1027–200	0.56846422	0.28919387	0.47529505	0.00772078	0.08786795
1027–500	0.66112025	0.20302145	0.4674717	0.00977301	0.09885856

Table 5.
Summary with the best results of similarity.

Collection-iterations	Best	Worst	Mean	Variance	Deviation
50–100	2	10	4.31578947	6.22105263	2.49420381
50–200	2	4	3	0.89210526	0.94451324
50–500	2	6	3.94736842	2.36578947	1.53811231
647–100	3	49	18.0526316	221.207895	14.8730594
647–200	2	67	18.9473684	305.831579	17.488041
647–500	2	73	23.2105263	426.368421	20.6486905
1027–100	2	110	31.2631579	1066.82895	32.6623475
1027–200	2	69	22.1052632	355.884211	18.8648936
1027–500	2	123	31	1179.21053	34.3396349

Table 6.
Summary with the best results of clusters.

Table 5 shows the results obtained with configurations: the best, worst, average, variance, and standard deviation of $f(x)$ over the 20 executions of the algorithm (**Table 6**).

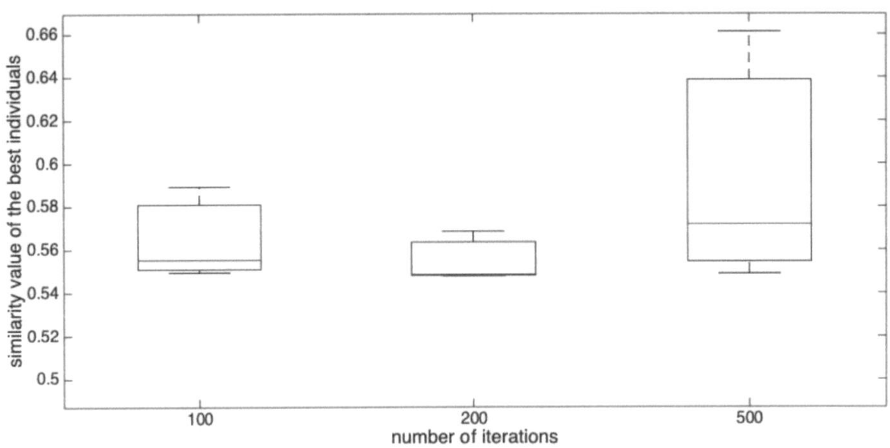

Figure 9.
Comparison of similarity between the best solutions found with 1027 services.

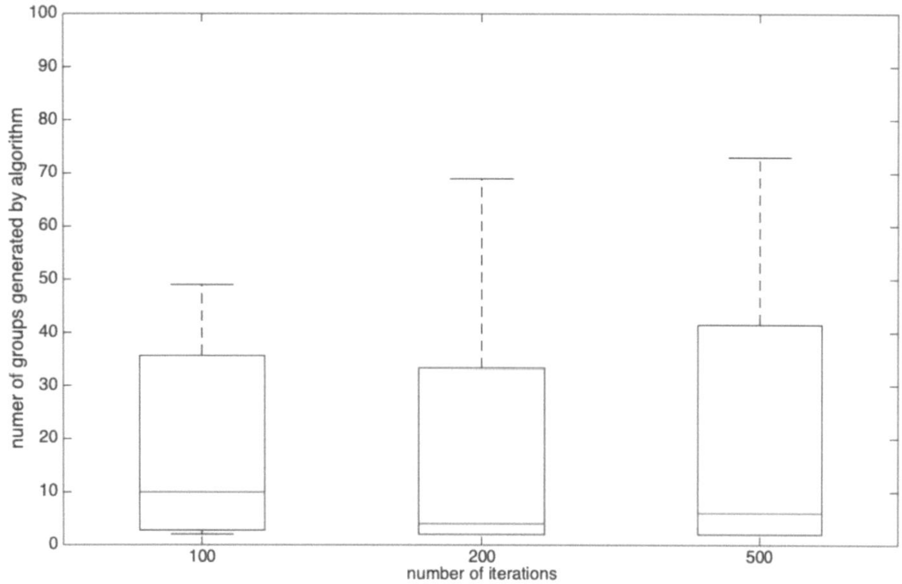

Figure 10.
Comparison of the number of groups in the best case for 1027 services.

Figures 9 and **10** show a comparison of results obtained from the algorithm with 100, 200, and 500 iterations of the instance of 1027 services. It can be seen that the best values of $f(x)$ are produced with 500 iterations; however the result of the number of groups involved is more stable and better with 200 iterations.

8. Conclusions

This chapter describes a hybrid algorithm for Web services clustering; the approach is based on the ABC optimization algorithm combined with the K-means and Consensus. The clustering process starts from the extraction and processing of WSDL documents, then the calculation of semantic similarities between pairs of Web services operations. The semantic similarity measurements are based on WordNet, combining corpus-based and taxonomic approaches. As a result of the calculations, eight matrices are generated which are the input data set to the hybrid bio-inspired algorithm.

Biologically inspired algorithms offer advantages over conventional clustering methods, such as the ability to find a near optimal solution by updating the candidate solutions iteratively and have self-organizing behavior.

The clustering algorithm designed is based on the behavior of the bees but was improved by incorporating K-means and Consensus so that the algorithm adjusts itself in each iteration. A series of experiments were conducted with the hybrid ABC algorithm, using optimal values for each adjustable parameter. The experiments were carried out with three collections with 50, 647, and 1027 Web services, and the algorithm was executed with variants of 100, 200, and 500 iterations. The hybrid ABC algorithm has shown good results for Web services clustering.

As future work, more combinations of semantic similarities, as well as incorporating more information of the description of the services and the data types incorporated in the XML service definitions.

Also the incorporation of other bio-inspired algorithms (swarm intelligence) for the classification and clustering of Web services, such as Particle Swarm Optimization (PSO), Bat Algorithm (BA), and Bird Swarm Algorithm (BSA).

Author details

Maricela Bravo*, Román A. Mora-Gutiérrez and Luis F. Hoyos-Reyes
Autonomous Metropolitan University, Ciudad de México, México

*Address all correspondence to: mcbc@azc.uam.mx

References

[1] Liang Q, Li P, Hung PC, Wu X. Clustering web services for automatic categorization. In: SCC'09: IEEE International Conference on Services Computing. IEEE; 2009. pp. 380-387

[2] Platzer C, Rosenberg F, Dustdar S. Web service clustering using multidimensional angles as proximity measures. ACM Transactions on Internet Technology. 2009;**9**(3):11

[3] Pop CB, Chifu VR, Salomie I, Dinsoreanu M, David T, Acretoaie V, et al. Biologically-inspired clustering of semantic web services. Birds or ants intelligence? Concurrency and Computation: Practice and Experience. 2012;**24**(6):619-633

[4] Du YY, Zhang YJ, Zhang XL. A semantic approach of service clustering and web service discovery. Information Technology Journal. 2013;**12**(5):967-974

[5] Wu J, Chen L, Zheng Z, Lyu MR, Wu Z. Clustering web services to facilitate service discovery. Knowledge and Information Systems. 2014;**38**(1): 207-229

[6] Prakash J, Singh PK. Evolutionary and swarm intelligence methods for partitional hard clustering. In: 2014 International Conference on Information Technology (ICIT). IEEE; 2014. pp. 264-269

[7] Sahoo G. A two-step artificial bee colony algorithm for clustering. Neural Computing and Applications. 2017; **28**(3):537-551

[8] Kotekar S, Kamath SS. Enhancing web service discovery using meta heuristic CSO and PCA based clustering. In: Progress in Intelligent Computing Techniques: Theory, Practice, and Applications. Singapore: Springer; 2018. pp. 393-403

[9] Fellbaum C. WordNet: An Electronic Lexical Database. Cambridge, MA: MIT Press; 1998

[10] Lesk M. Automatic sense disambiguation using machine readable dictionaries: How to tell a pine cone from an ice cream cone. In: Proceedings of SIGDOC '86. 1986

[11] Banerjee S, Pedersen T. An adapted Lesk algorithm for word sense disambiguation using WordNet. In: Computational Linguistics and Intelligent Text Processing. Berlin Heidelberg: Springer; 2002. pp. 136-145

[12] Wu Z, Palmer M. Verbs semantics and lexical selection. In: Proceedings of the 32nd Annual Meeting on Association for Computational Linguistics. Association for Computational Linguistics; 1994. pp. 133-138

[13] Resnik P. Using information content to evaluate semantic similarity. In: Proceedings of the 14th International Joint Conference on Artificial Intelligence. Montreal; 1995. pp. 448-453

[14] Jiang JJ, Conrath DW. Semantic similarity based on corpus statistics and lexical taxonomy. In: Proceedings of International Conference on Research in Computational Linguistics, Taiwan. 1997

[15] Lin D. An information-theoretic definition of similarity. In: Proceedings of the 15th International Conf. on Machine Learning. San Francisco, CA: Morgan Kaufmann; 1998. pp. 296-304

[16] Hirst G, St-Onge D. Lexical Chains as Representations of Context for the Detection and Correction of Malapropisms; 1998. pp. 305-332

[17] Leacock C, Chodorow M. Combining local context and WordNet

similarity for word sense identification. In: WordNet: An Electronic Lexical Database. Vol. 49. 1998. pp. 265-283

[18] Karaboga D. An Idea Based on Honey Bee Swarm for Numerical Optimization. Vol. 200. Technical Report: tr06. Erciyes University, Engineering Faculty, Computer Engineering Department; 2005

[19] Karaboga D, Ozturk C. A novel clustering approach: Artificial Bee Colony (ABC) algorithm. Applied Soft Computing. 2011;**11**(1):652-657

Chapter 3

Smart Material Planning Optimization Problem Analysis

Rich C. Lee and Man-ser Jan

Abstract

Mostly, the concept of smart manufacturing is addressed based upon how to effectively facilitate the production activities by using the automation equipment; however, causing the fluctuation of production may frequently root to the uncertain incoming sales orders. These uncertain factors may be influenced by various economic parameters, such as changes within trade regulations, competitor innovations, and changes within the market. In order to reduce the difference between the forecasted demand versus actual demand and to minimize risk, these factors need to be taken into account and be fully investigated. The current widely applied forecast methods are factory capacity-driven and based on the trend against the activity history. When the uncertainty comes from the external, then the forecasts derived from these models cannot provide convincing insights to let the firms make decisions confidently. Many previous prestigious studies focused on the problem-solving optimization mathematic methods and articulated the causality among latent factors; few have addressed to a holistic framework that the firms can practice on. This study presents a clear operable step-by-step framework to manage and cushion the impact from the external uncertain factors. It also introduces three novel and feasible production planning models with the consideration of the economic parameters. The empirical case was a multi-nation machinery-making firm who has adopted the proposed framework to optimize the material forecasts pursuing their smart manufacturing goals.

Keywords: material planning, supply chain management, smart manufacturing, advanced analytics, AI application

1. Introduction

In the pursuit of smart manufacturing, to satisfy the customer needs with quality, responsiveness and cost-effectiveness become the major challenge of nowadays factories [1]. The market demands are uncertain [2] and prone to be influenced by the composite effects of the driven forces, including the following: **Market saturation**: most known potential customers have already had the similar kind of product, and the new market segments are still not thriving to prove be the promising revenue fountain [3]. **Product innovation**: the customers hardly pay more for these products with slim marginal utility [4]. **Product differentiation**: most product features are common with the rivals, and the price-cutting thus becomes the inevitable survival strategy [5]. **Rival initiative**: in facing the same situation of demand slump, all rivals are endeavoring to stimulate the demand on their products to gain the shrinking profit [6]. **Customized features**: in the business-to-business (B2B) model, the purpose-intended design is the key to make the customers' final product differentiable to their rivals. While in the business-to-consumer (B2C) market, the customers are willing to pay more for those personalized products [7].

To effectively fulfill the business model of uncertain sales orders ensuring the product responsive delivery, the factory must prepare adequate resources, including the material and the workforce in advance. The more prepared resources are in advance, the more cost will be incurred; thus the revenue shrinks [8]. In the manufacturing practice, the bill of material (BOM) is an information to keep the product structural data of materials, such as part numbers, the quantity of need, and the associated specification [9]. To manage the material requisition, the total material needed shall be aggregated by the queued sales orders; the minimal quantity of a material is the required product quantities multiply the usage of that material in the BOM, respectively. The supplier material replenishment schedule may not be equivalent to one another due to their various conditions of production and delivery [10]. In most cases, the procurement of material in an economic scale will impact the production cost. This implies that the factory needs provision more and in advance for those materials that have greater variability in delivering.

Of those manufacturing automation equipment products, the sales may not aware of the gaps between the customer's expectations and the equipment limitations, including the required working environment, the excess inputs, and the unsynchronized outputs to the next step of productions. The factory product development team must customize the equipment in order to fit in the customer's application. The dilemma is whether the development team just tweaks the design for this specific case or puts more efforts on triggering the whole engineering change process to enhance the product features. If the decision is to enhance the product, that means a new BOM will be created, and some parts must be replaced; inevitably, the development team will commence a series of rigorous test on this design change; some tests take time. Consequently, the objective of material planning is to find the appropriate cost-effective solution under the constraints of order fulfillment and economic scale of the procurement.

The objective of this chapter is to articulate how the firm's material forecasting under the uncertain business environment can be improved from both management and advanced analytics perspectives.

2. Framing the problem

Apparently, it is a challenge to articulate the overall processes in which the aforementioned uncertainties might occur. Without a comprehensive expression, the firm cannot effectively collaborate on and make contribution to solve the problem. Thus, this chapter applied the problem frame analysis framework to disclose the complexity of the material planning in this smart manufacturing theme. Through this framework, all task-related participants can elaborate their actions to improve the forecast within and also look the problems a bigger firm-level picture. Essentially, the material forecast is an overall optimization in the firm. Such an optimization requires the synergy of the participants through the analytical models among tasks.

The problem frame is a method often used in the requirement engineering to describe a complicated problem's boundary and analyze the mutual influences among the problem factors in rigorous mathematic logic expressions [11]. One of the advantages of applying this method is these mathematic logic expressions can be easily transformed into the analytical forecast models. But it also brings its major disadvantage that the problem frames are not friendly to the business process improvement. Therefore, this chapter seeks to describe the essential framework of the material planning problem (**Figure 1**) in a more intuitive fashion, by using an expanded "Business Process Model and Notation" (BPMN).

The sales orders usually are not placed at the same time, but in a certain "random" way instead. If the materials take longer time in preparation than the order requested delivery time, consequently, the requested orders cannot be fulfilled, and the business responsiveness (one of the essentials of the smart manufacturing) will be compromised. Therefore, the factory must procure these materials in advance based on the market forecast. This forecast must be able to reflect the confidence level on the estimated quantities of the following: (1) **Mature products**: the firm's major revenue source, with a long, steady predictable sales history, usually adopted by a solid customer base. (2) **Adaptive products**: these are the extended or enhanced version of mature products or the long tail ones. (3) **Long-tailed products**: used by the existing customers for a period of time, but the demand is getting slim. (4) **New products**: used as the market penetration tool to explore the niche market.

Each product type may share common parts (materials) with one another. For example, if a new product is an enhanced version of the existing mature product, it will share many common parts with its predecessor. As product versions upgraded, a long-tailed product line is formed, the common parts usually will gradually decrease through generations. To keep as many common parts as possible in the new product design so that the material requisition planning can be further optimized is the key to lower the overstock risk. Nevertheless, in many occasions, the suppliers may discontinue to supply their legacy materials that will force the firm to change the design accordingly.

After the material preparation process completes, the inventory should be adequate to support the following procedures, including the production, shipping products as the sales orders requested, and deploying the products to the customers.

Formula (1) depicts the $qty(i)_{sales}$ which is the total requested quantity of a product aggregated from a group of sales orders; **Formula (2)** depicts the $qty(i)_{forecast}$ which consists of two parts, namely $qty(i)_{mature}$ and $qty(i)_{new}$; and **Formula (3)** depicts the $qty(i)_{total}$ which is the overall quantity at that batch. It is worth noting that the $qty(i)_{mature}$ can be either subjectively determined by the executives or conformed by a series of probabilistic-driven formulae over time.

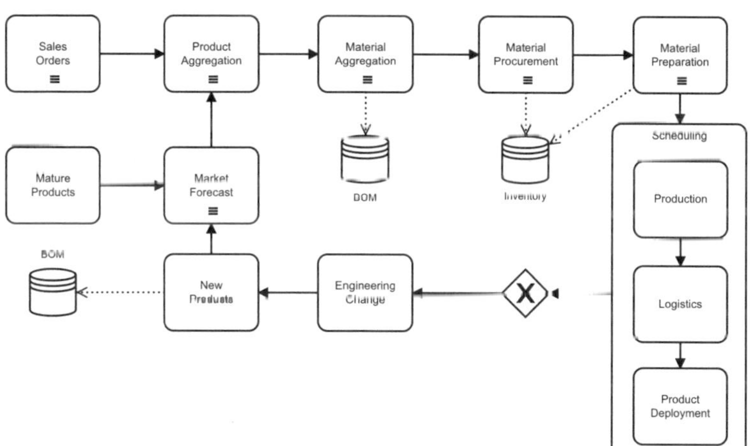

Figure 1.
Material planning problem frame.

The material aggregation is to calculate the required quantity for each material in the BOM; this chapter uses the column vector notation of $X_i = \left[x_{1\cdots p} \in P_i\right]$ to represent the materials that belong to the product P_i. Thus, the total required material quantities to fulfill the batch is also a column vector of $qty(i)_{total} * X_i$. Let X_i^s represents the quantities of these materials in the stock; therefore, the batch demand of these materials is $qty(i)_{total} * X_i - X_i^s$. But it is common that the material procurement should be in an economic scale denoted as X_i^p; the factor often considers the minimal purchase quantity for an order, the strategy of quantity-price advantage, and the safety quantity in stock. **Formula (4)** shows the total procured quantities of the materials in that batch which is a column vector of X_i^r:

$$qty(i)_{sales} = \sum_{j=1}^{n} \left(order_{i,j}\right) \tag{1}$$

$$qty(i)_{forecast} = qty(i)_{mature} + qty(i)_{new} \tag{2}$$

$$qty(i)_{total} = qty(i)_{sales} + qty(i)_{forecast} \tag{3}$$

$$X_i^r = \min\left[qty(i)_{total} * X_i - X_i^s, X_i^p\right] \tag{4}$$

Using common parts across the BOMs is a key to manage the risk and costs; this means, in the simplest case of two products P_i and P_j, the common parts X_{ij} will exist in the material vectors X_i and X_j. Either of the $qty(i)_{forecast}$ does not occur, and more $qty(j)_{sales}$ arrive or customers cancel orders causing the $qty(i)_{sales}$ drops and $qty(j)_{forecast}$ is doing well beyond the expectation, the X_{ij} can be used to support the business. The worst case is neither sales orders arrive, nor the forecasted market blooms as expected. The more common parts of X_{ij} have, the more flexible the product will be.

Furthermore, in some cases, the material x_i is a substitutable part-set with priorities, $x_i = \left\{x_i^k, k = 1\cdots m\right\}$, and usually, the priority implies the material received order, first-in-first-served (FIFS), or the release versions of parts, which serves the lower version part first. It will make the material planning more challenge when those legacy products are still in service at the customers' sites.

3. Supply chain optimization

In the smart manufacturing theme, the production planning is a multiperiod, multiproduct problem; the factory makes appropriate schedules based on a scenario tree containing all possible combinations to build the products optimally under the resource constraints. Both demand and supply uncertainties are driven by dynamic stochastic processes. The optimality is to satisfy the minimal resource consumed and the stochastic uncertainty of changes [12]. When multiple manufacturers at different sites collaborate to build products, the uncertainty may root from various external changes, illustrated in **Table 1**.

This problem can be resolved as multiobjective linear programming functions to minimize the total costs of supply chain and the total order fulfillment gaps across the factory sites [13]. However, both aforementioned approaches did not answer the fundamental question: how to determine the uncertainty of each forecast? This uncertainty causing the poor performance may be attributed from (1) over- or underprovisions on the different market demand prospects; (2) planning with the limited information; (3) misperception of customers' operating environment; and (4) quality of decision-making [14]. Therefore, this chapter incorporates the concepts from the multiobjective method with the consideration of overcoming the information asymmetry to present a novel approach as follows to tackle the problem.

Source of change	Reasons
Workforce size	The suppliers shrank their operation and impacted the replenishment, or the workers went on the strike
Production rate	Additional or unexpected cost incurred, the suppliers increased their material prices, or the rival lowered down their market prices
Seasonal overstocked	Based on the previous experience on business cycle, the firms had overprovisioned their resources than expected
Back orders	The suppliers canceled the procurement orders owing to their poor capacity planning, or the customers postponed the purchase plans for business reasons; and these numbers were counted in the forecast
Regulations	The authorities imposed new regulations that increased the firm additional costs, such as taxation or the equipment replacement
Extreme weather	There is no doubt that the extreme weather, including heavy snow, flood, or tsunami, has impacted the economic growth globally

Table 1.
The uncertain change sources.

The participants in the supply chain can reach the consensus about the market demand prospects of coming period, if information visibility is improved. This improved visibility will also relieve the information asymmetry side effect on the participants' planning. Fully documented product specifications and well-trained field engineers will overcome the deployment obstacles at customers' operating environment. The consented market demand prospect and the visible information are the tangible artifacts of the decision-making which is a collaborative process within the factory's departments and even with the external participants of the supply chain. Therefore, the more effective collaboration in improving the quality of decision-making, the less uncertainty bias shall be incurred.

4. Collaborative decision-making

The objective of conducting the collaborative decision-making process is to reach the consensus on the scale of the demand forecast in the next period. The diversity of this collaborative team is essential. The team members should cover the roles from (1) **material planner**, to report the current inventory status; (2) **procurement**, to report the collected forecasts from the suppliers; (3) **sales**, to present the products' front log with their selling confidence levels for each customer, respectively; (4) **channel**, to present the products' front log with their selling confidence levels for each distributor, respectively; (5) **marketing**, to disclose the overall demand from the external professional analysis and the competitor's recent launched initiatives; (6) **finance**, to present the current cash flow status and the capital capacity of procurement and suggest the forecast quantity based on the analysis of management accounting; and (7) **data analyst**, a critical role in the forecasting under the uncertainty, who designs the analytical process, including constructing the optimization formulae, collecting and compiling the datasets, disclosing the insight about how and where the inaccuracy of previous forecasts came from, and, the most importantly, making the prediction closer to the coming business reality.

Figure 2 illustrates this collaborative decision process; after the group decision reaches the consensus on the material planning, the participants draft a couple of proposals and submit it to the material planning committee composed of the firm executives, the decision group participants, and the external industry professionals.

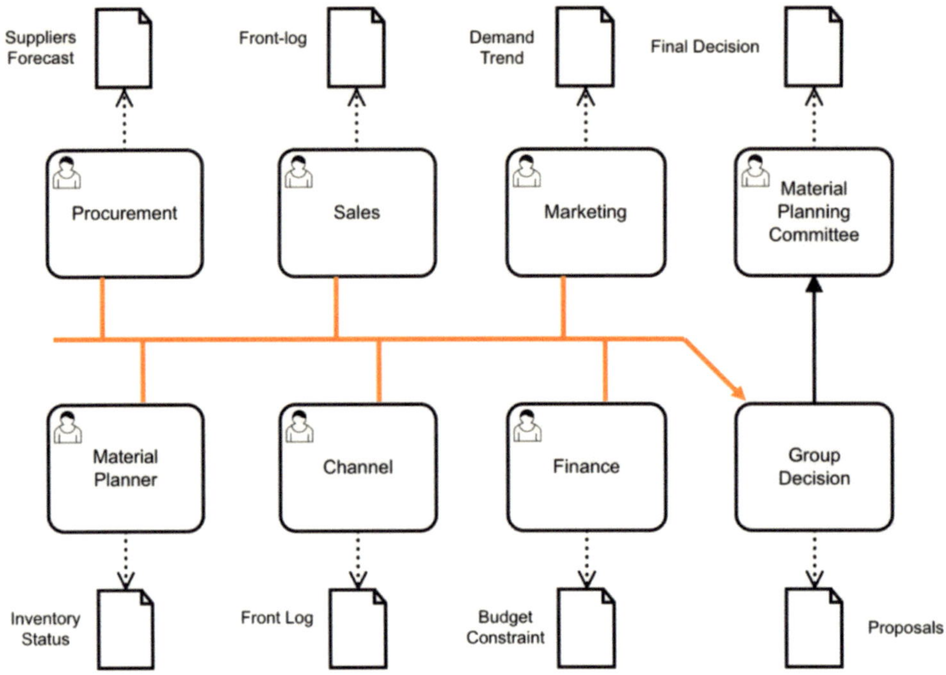

Figure 2.
Collaborative decision process.

The committee will make the final decision on the material planning. It is worth noting that the data analyst plays the backbone role facilitating the tasks of other participants throughout the process.

5. Effective elaboration

To make the aforementioned collaboration more effectively to elaborate the material planning proposals, this chapter presents a generic form for the group decision participants to discuss with. **Table 2** illustrates a sample form for the forecasting. The form consists of two portions, the target product and its critical components.

In this sample form, the product *PD* portion, which belongs to *CA* category, currently has *PI* units in stock, its last period's turnover rate ($\Delta out/\Delta in$) is *PT*, the maximal can-build quantity is *BQ* units under current on hand material status, previous forecast accuracy rates, calculated by $\left(F_{previous} - \widehat{F_{actual}}\right)/\widehat{F_{actual}}$, were *AM*, *AS*, *AC*, *AP*, and *AF*, and the forecasted quantities are *FM*, *FS*, *FC*, *FP*, and *FF*.

Category/product		Inventory	Turnover	Build/suppler	Accuracy/forecast		Source
CA	**PD**	**PI**	**PT**	**BQ**	**AM**	**FM**	**Marketing**
MR_1		MI_1	MT_1	MS_1	AS	FS	Sales
MR_2		MI_2	MT_2	MS2	AC	FC	Channels
MR_3		MI_3	MT_3	MS_3	AP	FP	Suppliers
MR_4		MI_4	MT_4	MS_4	AF	FF	Finance

Table 2.
Material forecast sample form.

The critical components section contains four major parts—$MR_{1...4}$, inventory levels are denoted by $MI_{1...4}$, turnover rates denoted by $MT_{1...4}$, and the suppliers of critical components are denoted by $MS_{1...4}$ respectively. It is worth noting that all the figures in the form depend on the information capability of firm, especially the *BQ* quantity which must be iteratively calculated during the process.

The final agreed decision on the forecast of the product can be systematically measured by **Formula (5)**. The outer summation adds up the forecast of the five groups and multiplies by their w_i weights, respectively. The inner summation adds up the group's forecast decision. Each group has the p_i participants, and there is also a θ_j weight for every participant's $forecast_{i,j}$ quantity:

$$Forecast_{final} = \sum_{i=1}^{5} \left[w_i \sum_{j=1}^{p_i} \left(\theta_j * forecast_{i,j} \right) \right] \tag{5}$$

The reason why previous forecast accuracy rates were excluded from $Forecast_{final}$ is because the participants will adjust their forecast rates accordingly, based on assigned weights by their group leaders. The purpose of this form is to give a template for the group discussion; it can help the participants make their forecasts not relying on the hunches but based on the fact of tangible numbers.

6. Material dynamics

The material readiness is essential to the production, especially for those scarce and/or valuable ones. There are several reasons causing the material scarcity: (1) usually these are subcomponents which required the outsourcing, customized design; (2) those materials are provided by the single source or the oligopoly market; and (3) the materials are common but essential in many products, and when these products are hot in the market, these materials become very difficult to acquire the adequate quantities to support the firm's production. To prevent the shortage of materials, reserving and maintaining the materials at some level of quantities in stock are common measures in practice.

The challenge of making the decision on the quantities of these safe stocks is that the procurement and the planner must be aware of the supply market's movements and take action in a proactive manner at all times. **Formula (6)** illustrates the general material acquired function; when qty_{need} is a negative value, it means the reserved stock is no longer able to support the production, and thus the further procurement is needed. Each material more or less will have waste during the production; it can be attributed to the poor quality or mishandling by the workers. The $\omega\%$ is the additional ratio—can be an average number from the past—to compensate the production loss. **Formula (7)** shows the total quantity of use qty_{use} which is the multiplication of the loss and the summation of total p forecast products' used quantities qty_i in BOM_i, respectively:

$$qty_{need} = qty_{stock} - \left(qty_{use} + qty_{safety} \right) \tag{6}$$

$$qty_{use} = (1 + \omega\%) \sum_{i=1}^{p} \left[qty_i * BOM_i \right] \tag{7}$$

$$qty_{safety} = MA\left(qty_{use}, \kappa \right) * \left(\frac{e^{-\mu} * \mu^{qty_{order}}}{qty_{order}!} \right) \tag{8}$$

The estimation of qty_{safety} plays a significant role in the forecast accuracy. If the safety stock is overestimated, it will incur the additional financial pressure or discontinues the production due to the shortage of supply if the safety stock is underestimated. This chapter proposes a generic function: $qty_{safety} = MA(qty_{use}, \kappa) * \varphi\%$, it is based on the moving-average of the material in the past κ terms and multiplied with a given weight for that material. Furthermore, **Formula (8)** presents more aggressive idea on the estimation of $\varphi\%$ by applying the Poisson probability distribution subject to the product orders that use this material [16, 17].

7. Uncertain demand

The "bullwhip effect" is a classic problem in the supply chain management; the obvious symptom is the overstocking in the whole supply chain. When the market demand declines not as the forecast expected, it will potentially impose the financial risk significantly. More overproduced products will push to the distribution channels, and the channels might sacrifice their margin in order to attract the consumers to buy more until the demand has saturated. Both the product and the material inventory levels will hike and thus incur the warehouse management cost and the value depreciation. This symptom will impact more when the optimistic supply chain tiers are deep. It is simply because the suppliers in each tier might magnify their forecasts under the asymmetric market demand information [18]. The root cause of this effect is that the market demand does not always follow the trend derived from the past. It is very challenging to forecast the demand of the individual product because the order quantity is slim. But the products in the same category may share a common component structure in the majority. In the configure-to-order model, let the consumer to optionally select the components from the configuration of the product; the differences among these products can be as simple as just a few components vary than one another [19]. This implies that the forecast model can be applied to reduce the inventory overstock and understock risk, as long as the quantity volatile product demands shares common materials.

The increasing economic disturbance such as the trade barriers has annoyingly amplified the market demand uncertainty. For instances, recently, the US-China trade tensions [20] and the Brexit [21] are the perfect examples of this. In order to assess business potential risk, we must consider the big picture and be aware of the impact of various economic parameter through the use of PEST analysis: (1) **political harmony**, such as shared visions, diplomatic situation, polarization; (2) **economic factors**, such as disposable income, interest rate, wealth inequality; (3) **social trend**, such as product adoption preferences, living style expectation, stability of community; and (4) **technology novelty**, such as the maturity of supply chain, innovation capability. Certainly, the firm can consider more perspectives than PEST or apply other perspectives that are more comprehensive to the firm's business environment.

This chapter proposes the material planning committee to set the confidence levels (a sort of weights) on these firm external perspectives to adjust the demand forecast. The p_i is the confidence level of a perspective; as **Formula (9)** suggests, $p_i \Downarrow$ is set when the committee think the forecast is too optimistic; or giving $p_i \Uparrow$ to amplify the scale of business otherwise. A new scoring scheme is presented in this chapter, as illustrated in **Formula (10)**:

$$p_i \in \Re, 0.0 < p_i \Downarrow < 1.0 < p_i \Uparrow < 2.0 \tag{9}$$

$$\tau(p) = \left[\sum_{i=1}^{n} p_i^{\ 2} + \sum_{i=1}^{n-1} \sum_{j=i+1}^{n-i} \left(p_i * p_j \right) \right] * \tau^{-1}(p = \{1.0_{1..n}\}) \tag{10}$$

where $\tau(p)$ is the forecast adjustment coefficient, $0.0 < \tau(p) < 2.0$. $p = \{1.0_{1..n}\}$ means the set containing n perspectives, and each $p_i = 1.0$ which is the expected value of no adjustment to the forecast.

8. Empirical case and discussion

The empirical case is about a global production automation equipment manufacturer. Their flag-fleet products are the Computer Numerical Control (CNC) category which is widely used in the production to provide more precise, complicated and repeatable control than just manning the equipment. Basically, each CNC consists of five major components: (1) input, receiving the signals/status from the controlled equipment via various handshaking interfaces; (2) output, sending a set of instructions to the equipment to proceed the next action; (3) control, a number of electrical mechanical units to convert or transform the input signals to the processor and translate the electrical magnetic signals into the output instruction set; (4) processor, performing the signal predefined computations accordingly; and (5) human, providing the interface, usually is through keypad panel, to let worker interact or intervene with the control process.

8.1 Economic parameter

The empirical case adopted the stock market performance information as their foundation of setting the $p_{economic}$ parameter, the most significant $w_{economic}$ among all perspectives in the PEST evaluation model. They posit that two stock indices, the NASDAQ and their major rival/benchmark in China, can reflect their business trend.

Figure 3 illustrates a sample economic factor parameter analysis against the stock performance of Nasdaq and the rival's in 2018. The X-axis is the dates and Y-axis is the standardized ratios. The stock index changed is $Scale = Stock_{Close} - Stock_{Open}$, and the maximal fluctuated is $Mag = Stock_{high} - Stock_{low}$. The standardization is to transform the indices in to the values between 0 and 1 by applying $[index - \min(index)]/[\max(index) - \min(index)]$.

Formula 11 defines a composite scoring function for the economic factors. The $\Delta Score_i$ is the first-order difference of the composite scores; by applying the product of these difference vectors, **Formula 12** derives each s_i in the evaluation vector S. The *trend*, showing both indices are moving toward the same direction, is the proportion of all positive s_i in S illustrated in **Formula 13**. Choosing the appropriate stock indices by the data analyst to reflect the current sector's business state will determine the usefulness of this *trend* function. **Formula 14** introduces the matrix cosine similarity method to facilitate this choosing process, especially in targeting the appropriate rivals in the volatile stock market. The committee can reference these figures to determine the comfortable $p_{economic}$ to fit in the group decision model:

$$Score_i = \sqrt{Scale_i^{\ 2} + Mag_i^{\ 2} + Volume_i^{\ 2}} \tag{11}$$

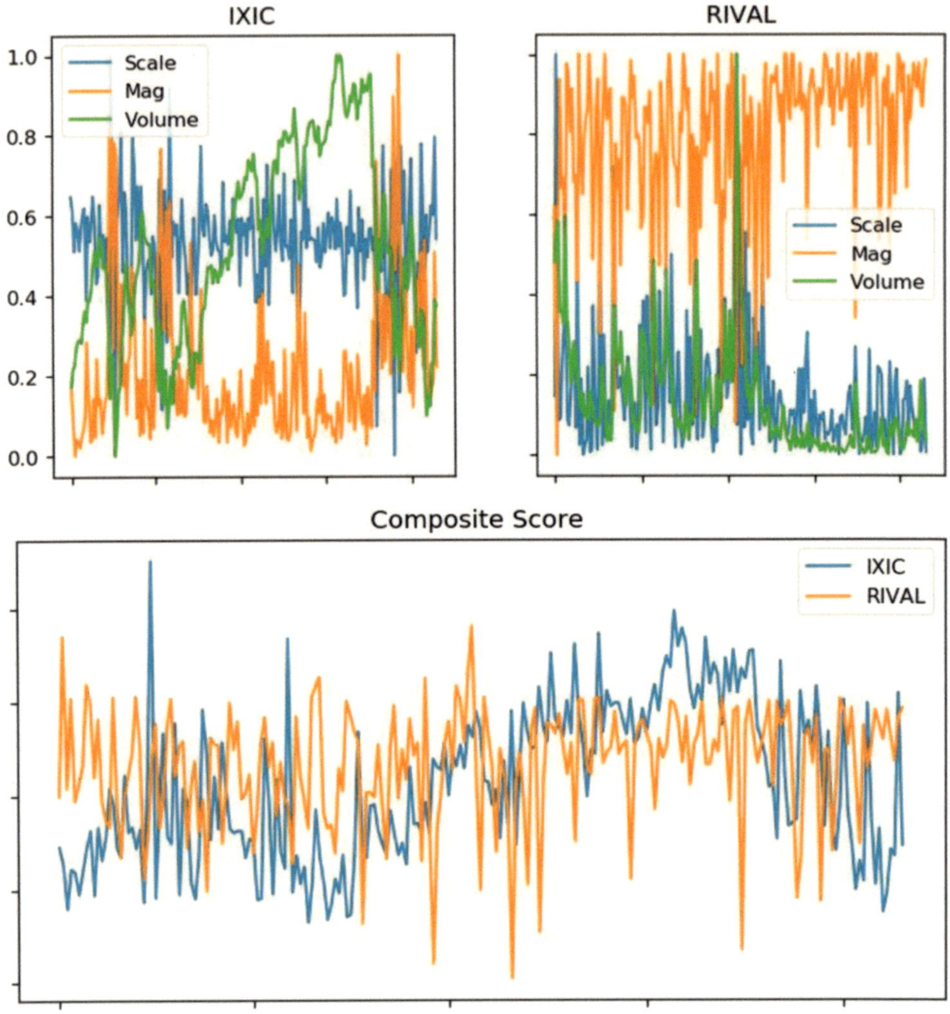

Figure 3.
A sample economic factor parameter analysis.

$$S = \prod_{i=1}^{2} (\Delta Score_i), s_i \in S \tag{12}$$

$$Trend = \frac{count(S, \forall s_i \geq 0)}{count(S)} \tag{13}$$

$$Similarity = 1 - \frac{Score_i^T * Score_j}{\|Score_i\| * \|Score_j\|} \tag{14}$$

8.2 Material requisition models

8.2.1 Fixed input

The proposed fixed input material requisition model (**Figure 5**) makes the following assumptions (1) suppose the sample material fulfillment lead time takes three terms (usually in weeks); (2) suppose the sample material economic scale of supply is 1000 units; (3) the predicted loss ratio is set on 5% of each procurement quantity; (4) when the inventory is below the safety stock, an economic scale purchase will be made; (5) when the inventory is short to fill the order, a purchase of the lead time multiply the economic scale will be made (3000 units in this model); and (6) the supplier will deliver the sample material after the lead time of the purchase.

In **Figure 4**, the sales orders related to this sample material have shown the demand, with the star markers, slumped from the expected 1000 units down to near 750. The triangle markers represent the purchases, and the round markers are the remained inventory. The green circle represents the stock on hand at the end of the forecast period. With the exception of the last circle (leftover stock), they coincide with every purchase made (triangle). By applying this model, the production may stop because of the material shortage; finding the sufficient safety stock quantity is a challenge to prevent the disruption of production:

$$params = \left(qty_{order}, qty_{Safety}, qty_{economic}, time_{lead}, qty_{loss}\right) \tag{15}$$

$$risk_{safety}, stop_{safety} = Model(params) \tag{16}$$

This chapter applies the iterative method by changing the qty_{Safety}, illustrated in **Formula 16**, and evaluating the return values. The $risk_{safety}$ is the occurrences when inventory is below the qty_{Safety}, and the $stop_{safety}$ is how many times that the product has stopped. The model function $Model(params)$ behavior depends on the settings of the given qty_{order}, $qty_{economic}$, $time_{lead}$, qty_{loss}, and the variable qty_{Safety}. In the sample material case, the minimal qty_{Safety} to prevent the disruption of product is 1000 units (coincidently matched with the $qty_{economic}$). It is worth noting that if the $qty_{economic}$ is underestimated, the production disruptions are inevitable in this fixed input model.

8.2.2 Variable input

An enhanced variable input of the material requisition model is illustrated in **Figure 5**. It has the same configuration as the fixed input, but (1) suppose the sample material economic scale of supply is per 1000-unit; (2) when the inventory is below the safety stock; an economic scale purchase will be made; (3) when the inventory is short to fill the order; a purchase of the lead time multiply the economic scale will be made; and (4) each purchased quantity will be based on the moving average of the quantities of the previous lead time of the orders, illustrated in

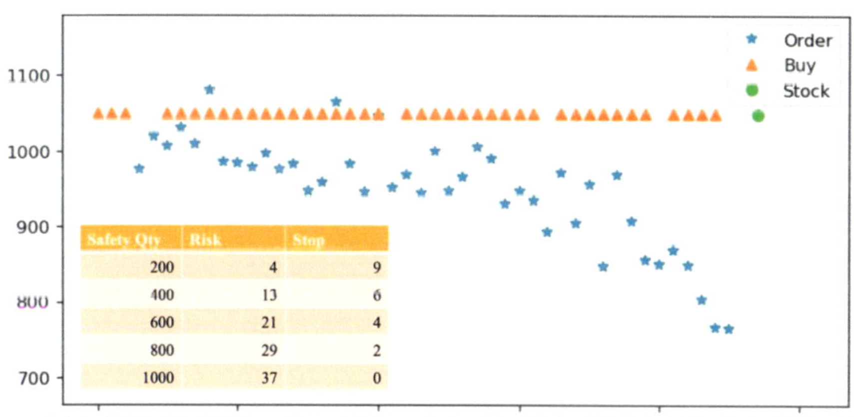

Safety Qty	Risk	Stop
200	4	9
400	13	6
600	21	4
800	29	2
1000	37	0

Figure 4.
Sample material fixed input requisition model.

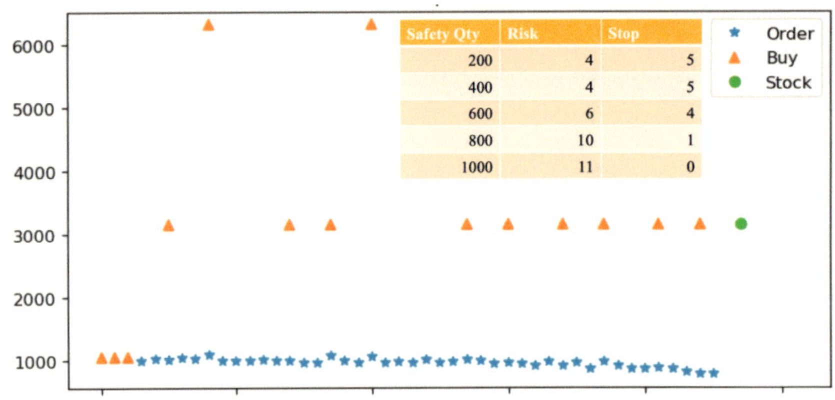

Figure 5.
Sample material variable input requisition model.

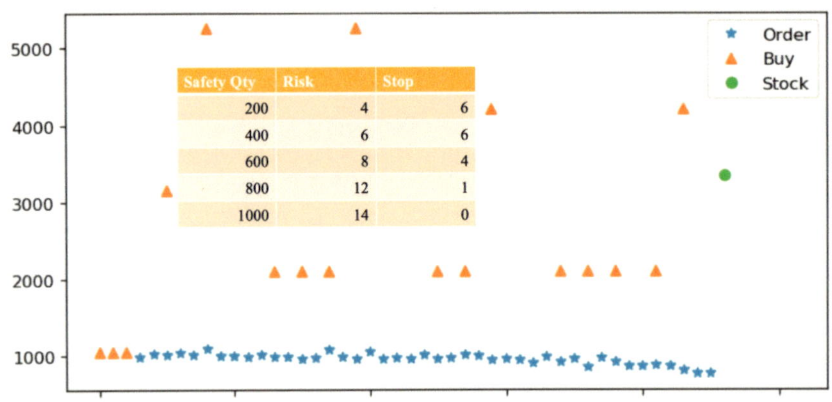

Figure 6.
Sample material trend variable input requisition model.

Formula 17. When qty_{Safety} is adequate, the purchase quantities are high, but the frequency is less; however, the production disruption will never occur in this variable input model.

$$qty_{purchase} = MA\left(qty_{use}, \kappa\right) * time_{lead} \tag{17}$$

8.2.3 Trend variable input

The final proposed model, illustrated in **Figure 6**, is based on the aforementioned variable input, but each purchased quantity will consider the trend about the previous lead time of qty_{order}. The simplest form of the trend function is shown in **Formula 18**, taking the $MA^{(1)}$ first-order derivative, and if the trend is positive (demand increasing), the purchase will plus one additional average quantity; if the trend is otherwise, the purchase will lessen one additional average quantity instead. Comparing this model with the aforementioned variable input, the inventory levels are constantly lower, and it implies the risk is also less in the case the demand drops drastically. For the long-term observed material, the trend can be estimated by a proper probability distribution or the decision of PEST:

$$qty_{purchase} = MA\left(qty_{use}, \kappa\right) * \left[time_{lead} + Trend\left(MA^{(1)}\left(qty_{use}, \kappa\right)\right)\right] \tag{18}$$

DOI: http://dx.doi.org/10.5772/intechopen.84614

9. Conclusion

The customers buying preferences stimulate and inspire a new way of manufacturing. It has been a trend that the manufacturers are heading toward their ultimate goals of smart manufacturing. Many firms put the equipment automation as the first step of their smart manufacturing initiatives. But soon they found out that the current business challenge is on the uncertain market demand rather than just focusing on the operation automation. In addition, the smart manufacturing initiative is a sort of business reengineering process; it requires all participants to be aware in the problems in a holistic view. This is where this chapter would like to address.

In the smart manufacturing theme, the material planning is a challenging task under the uncertain demand environment. The task is not just the responsibility of the planner nor the data analyst but the synergy of all related participants. This chapter presents three material requisition models, for those materials having short lead times or being able to apply the pull model (vendor managed inventory, VMI), the fixed input model is adequate enough; for those materials having the same trend for a period of time, the variable input model can compensate the trend difference and prevent the excessive purchase; and for those volatile demand materials, the trend variable input model has the lowest inventory level than the others.

Finally, all proposed modes treat the loss ratio $\omega\%$ as constant for easy to explain, and this ratio should be measured from the production. To manufacture smarter products nowadays, to create a healthy collaborative culture within the firm is above all to enhance the competence of data analysis, and to improve the information systems is the cornerstone of survival and the business success as well.

Author details

Rich C. Lee* and Man-ser Jan
Institute of Applied Economics, National Taiwan Ocean University, Taiwan, China

*Address all correspondence to: richchihlee@gmail.com

References

[1] Kusiak A. Smart manufacturing. International Journal of Production Research. 2018;**56**(1–2):508-517

[2] Li S. A structural model of productivity, uncertain demand, and export dynamics. Journal of International Economics. 2018;**115**:1-15

[3] Anisimov VG, Anisimov EG, Saurenko TN, Sonkin MA. The model and the planning method of volume and variety assessment of innovative products in an industrial enterprise. Journal of Physics: Conference Series. 2017;(1):803

[4] Truong Y, Klink RR, Simmons G, Grinstein A, Palmer M. Branding strategies for high-technology products: The effects of consumer and product innovativeness. Journal of Business Research. 2017;**70**(70):85-91

[5] Luan YJ. Forecasting marketing-mix responsiveness for new products. Journal of Marketing Research. 2010; **47**(3):444-457

[6] Harmeling CM, Moffett JW, Arnold MJ, Carlson BD. Toward a theory of customer engagement marketing. Journal of the Academy of Marketing Science. 2017;**45**(3):312-335

[7] Modrak V. An introduction to mass customized manufacturing. In: Mass Customized Manufacturing: Theoretical Concepts and Practical Approaches. 2017. pp. 21-32

[8] VafaArani H, VafaArani SA, Torabi H. Integrated material-financial supply chain master planning under mixed uncertainty. Information Sciences. 2018; **423**:96-114

[9] Ivanov D, Alexander T, Schönberger J. Production and material requirements planning. Global Supply Chain and Operations Management. 2017:317-343

[10] Paul SK, Asian S, Goh M, Torabi SA. Managing sudden transportation disruptions in supply chains under delivery delay and quantity loss. Annals of Operations Research. 2017:1-32

[11] Hall JG, Rapanotti L, Jackson M. Problem frame semantics for software development. Software and Systems Modeling. 2005;**4**(2):189-198

[12] Zanjani MK, Nourelfath M, Aït-Kadi D. A multi-stage stochastic programming approach for production planning with uncertainty in the quality of raw materials and demand. International Journal of Production Research. 2010;**48**(16):4701-4723

[13] Al-e-Hashem SM, Malekly H, Aryanezhad M. A multi-objective robust optimization model for multi-product multi-site aggregate production planning in a supply chain under uncertainty. International Journal of Production Economics. 2011;**134**:28-42

[14] Simatupang MT, Sridharan R. The collaborative supply chain. The International Journal of Logistics Management. 2002;**13**(1):15-30

[15] Ponte B, Sierra E, Fuente DD, Lozano J. Exploring the interaction of inventory policies across the supply chain: An agent-based approach. Computers & Operations Research. 2017;**78**:335-348

[16] Schuster M, Minner S, Tancrez J-S. Two-stage supply chain design with safety stock placement decisions. International Journal of Production Economics. 2019;**209**:183-193

[17] Schmitt TG, Kumar S, Stecke KE, Glover FW, Ehlen MA. Mitigating disruptions in a multi-echelon supply chain using adaptive ordering. Omega. 2016;**68**:185-198

[18] Chen F, Drezner Z, Ryan JK, Simchi-Levi D. Quantifying the bullwhip effect in a simple supply chain: The impact of forecasting, lead times, and information. Management Science. 2000;**46**(3):436-443

[19] Gunasekaran A, Ngai E. Build-to-order supply chain management: A literature review and framework for development. Journal of Operations Management. 2005;**23**(5):423-451

[20] Goto S. What do US-China tensions mean for Asia? In: World Economic Forum, International Trade and Investment. 2018

[21] Breene K. What would Brexit Mean for the UK Economy. In: World Economic Forum, European Union. 2016

Chapter 4

A Deep Learning-Based Aesthetic Surgery Recommendation System

Phan Chau Phuc Thinh, Bui Thi Xuyen,
Nguyen Do Trung Chanh, Dao Huu Hung
and Mimura Daisuke

Abstract

We propose in this chapter a deep learning-based recommendation system for aesthetic surgery, composing of a mobile application and a deep learning model. The deep learning model built based on the dataset of before- and after-surgery facial images can estimate the probability of the perfection of some parts of a face. In this study, we focus on the most two popular treatments: rejuvenation treatment and eye double-fold surgery. It is assumed that the outcomes of our history surgeries are perfect. Firstly a convolutional autoencoder is trained by eye images before and after surgery captured from various angles. The trained encoder is utilized to extract learned generic eye features. Secondly, the encoder is further trained by pairs of image samples, captured before and after surgery, to predict the probability of perfection, so-called perfection score. Based on this score, the system would suggest whether some sorts of specific aesthetic surgeries should be performed. We preliminarily achieve 88.9 and 93.1% accuracy on rejuvenation treatment and eye double-fold surgery, respectively.

Keywords: aesthetic surgery, rejuvenation treatment, eye double-fold surgery, recommendation system, convolutional neural network, autoencoder

1. Introduction

Plastic surgery is a surgical specialty relating to restoration, reconstruction, or alteration of the human body. There are two major categories: (1) reconstructive surgery and (2) aesthetic or cosmetic surgery. The former is intended to correct dysfunctional areas of the body and is reconstructive in nature. Examples of this kind include breast reconstruction, burn repair surgery, congenital defect repair, lower extremity reconstruction, hand surgery, scar revision surgery, etc. The latter focuses on enhancing the appearance of the patient. Improving aesthetic appeal, symmetry, and proportion are among the key goals. The scope of aesthetic surgery procedures includes breast enhancement, facial contouring, facial rejuvenation, body contouring, skin rejuvenation, etc. The scope of this chapter restricts to the latter, aesthetic surgery.

In aesthetic surgery, the treated areas function properly; it is optional based on the willingness of the patient who cares about their beauty. The sense of beauty also varies from geographical areas and sometimes follows either local or global fashion trends. Therefore, the consultation in aesthetic surgery of experienced doctors is extremely important. The severe problem of population aging in developed countries leads to the shortage of high-skill labors in almost all industrial sectors. Thus this chapter proposes a deep learning-based aesthetic surgery recommendation system, aiming at keeping the valuable know-how of experienced doctors to consult the patient in aesthetic surgery. Moreover, the continuous learning capability of the AI model also facilitates the self-update of the newly fashionable know-how in this field, given a set of rich training data.

Although aesthetic surgery can be performed on all areas of the head, neck, and body, our focused areas in this chapter are the facial area. We take the most popular treatments for facial areas, rejuvenation, and eye double-fold surgery into consideration. In order to build a deep learning system which is capable of predicting the perfection of aesthetic surgery, we collect an in-house training dataset composing of pairs of images capturing the eye area of the same person before and after aesthetic surgery. It is assumed that the beauty of facial areas after surgery is perfect, that is, the know-how of an aesthetic surgeon is embedded into these pairs of images.

In order to keep the know-how of experienced aesthetic surgeon, we propose to train a deep neural network by these pairs of images in our in-house dataset. Among various kinds of neural network architectures, proposed in the literature, convolutional neural networks (CNN) have been demonstrating outstanding performance in image recognition [1]. This was the first time a large and deep CNN—AlexNet model—achieved record-breaking results on highly challenging image recognition dataset with a margin of more than 10% with respect to the second best which makes use of handcrafted features. Even though the performance of AlexNet is still far from the inferotemporal pathway of the human visual system, it created the way of success for successor models such as Inception [2], VGG [3], and Resnet [4]. The convolutional layers learn from data to extract a rich set of features for a variety of purposes such as image classification and recognition [4], visual tracking [5], face recognition [6], object detection [7], person reidentification [8], etc. The power of CNN is enabled by the learning mechanism in which weights of convolutional filters are adjusted toward the adaption to the labels. The generalization of CNN is guaranteed by the availability of a huge dataset to produce an outstanding performance on unseen data.

However, our in-house dataset is not huge enough to guarantee the generalization of CNN for this task. Therefore, we propose to use convolutional autoencoder neural networks to overcome the limitation of our small dataset. The network is firstly trained in a layer-wise mechanism to reconstruct input images in the output layer. This training mechanism is completely unsupervised. After the convolutional autoencoder neural network is trained, the decoder part is truncated. Only the encoder part is kept and is concatenated with fully connected layers. The whole network will be trained by images and their labels, before and after surgery. The weights of the encoder parts are kept intact because the encoder parts have already learned the key features of the training image set. As a result, our proposed model is able to achieve 88.9 and 93.1% accuracy on rejuvenation treatment and eye double-fold surgery, respectively.

The rest of this chapter is organized as follows. Section 2 describes our contribution to the backdrop of related work. The proposed method is presented in detail in Section 3. Finally, we conclude the chapter and delineate future work in Section 4.

2. Related work

The number of aesthetic surgery, particularly for facial areas, has been recently drastically surged. This trend even could spread further in the next few years due to lowering the average cost of such treatments and the desire of beautification. Numerous research works have been proposed in the literature, especially in the computer vision community to address the challenges posed by aesthetic surgery. These research works are generally broken into three categories, namely, skin quality inspection, face recognition after surgery, and surgery planning and recommendation.

Aesthetic surgery in facial areas to correct facial feature anomaly and to improve the beauty, in general, alters the original facial information. It poses a significant challenge for face recognition algorithms. Majority of proposed methods in the literature focused on the advances of handcraft features. Richa et al. [9] have investigated the effects of aesthetic surgery to face recognition. Amal et al. [10] proposed a face recognition system based on LBP and GIST descriptor to address this problem. Maria et al. [11] combine two methods, face recognition against occlusions and expression variations (FARO) [12] and face analysis for commercial entities (FACE) [13] with split face architecture to deal with the effects of plastic surgery to process each face region as separate biometrics. For a comprehensive survey of face recognition algorithms against variations due to aesthetic surgery, please refer to [14].

Skin quality inspection and assessment is also a potential application of computer vision and deep learning methods. By assessing skin quality, it is able to help the aesthetic surgeon to recommend certain kinds of operation to enhance the beauty of the face. Surface roughness, wrinkle depth, volume, and epidermal thickness of the skin are quantitatively computed by applying deep learning method to images captured by optical coherence tomography [15]. The facial skin is classified into facial skin patches, namely, normal, spots, and wrinkles, by using convolutional neural networks [16]. Batool and Chellappa [17] proposed a method to model wrinkles as texture features or curvilinear objects, so-called aging skin texture, for facial aging analysis. They reviewed commonly used image features to capture the intensity gradients caused by facial wrinkles, such as Laplacian of Gaussian, Hessian filter, steerable filter bank, Gabor filter bank, active appearance model, and local binary patterns.

In the last category of aesthetic surgery planning and recommendation, facial beauty prediction is the first step to assess whether or not a face should perform an aesthetic surgery. Yikui et al. [18] described BeautyNet in which multiscale CNN is employed to obtain deep features, characterizing the facial beauty, and is combined with transfer learning strategy to alleviate overfitting and to achieve robust performance on unconstrained faces. Lu et al. [19] transferred rich deep features from a pretrained VGG16 model on face verification task to Bayesian ridge regression algorithms for predicting facial beauty.

Going beyond the facial beauty prediction, Arakawa and Nomoto [20] removed wrinkles and spots while preserving natural skin roughness by using a bank of nonlinear filters for facial beautification. Eighty-four facial landmark points are represented in a vector of 234 normalized lengths to compare with vectors of beautiful faces to suggest how to warp the triangulation of the original face to the beautiful ones [21]. Bottino et al. [22] presented a quantitative approach to automatically recommend effective patient-specific improvements of facial attractiveness by comparing the face of the patient with a large database of attractive faces. Simulations are performed by applying features of similar attractive faces into the patient faces with a suitable morphing of facial shape.

Our research differs from the above-related works in two senses. Firstly, a convolutional autoencoder is employed to learn rich features and characterize both unattractive and beautiful faces in an unsupervised manner, rather than under supervised learning [18, 19]. The learned features are more discriminative than handcrafted features [9–13, 15–17]. Secondly, the proposed deep learning framework facilitates a holistic approach to identify what kinds of facial treatment should be performed to enhance the attractiveness, rather than predicting beauty score [20–22].

3. Method

The method is divided into two main steps, namely, train feature extractor and train classification model as shown in **Figure 1**. The dataset is first utilized to train the feature extraction model based on convolutional autoencoder. In this step, the convolutional autoencoder is trained in order to learn to encode the input in a set of images and then tries to reconstruct the input from them. Thus, it can learn the feature of the input data by minimizing the reconstruction error. Then we extract the encoder and use it as the feature extractor.

Figure 2 illustrates the method of training feature extractor. From the first step, the model is trained only to learn filters able to extract feature that can be used to reconstruct the input. These filters in the encoder then are extracted and then utilized as the feature extraction for the classification model which is a fully connected layer.

3.1 Feature extractor

Autoencoders are well-known unsupervised learning algorithm whose original purpose is to find latent lower-dimensional state spaces of datasets, but they are also capable of solving other problems, such as image denoising, enhancement, or colorization. The main idea behind autoencoders is to reduce the input into a latent state space with lower dimensions and then try to reconstruct the input from this representation. Thus the autoencoder uses its input as the reference of the output in the learning phase. The two parts are called encoder and decoder, respectively. By reducing the number of variables which represent the data, we force the model to learn how to keep only meaningful information, from which the input is reconstructable. It can also be viewed as a compression technique as shown in **Figure 2**.

A conventional autoencoder is composed of two layers, corresponding to the encoder $f_w(.)$ and decode $g_v(.)$. It aims to find a code for each input that minimizes the difference between input, x_i, and output, $g_u(f_W(x_i))$, over all samples [23]:

$$\min_{W,U} \frac{1}{n} \sum_{i=1}^{n} \left\| g_u(f_W(x_i)) - x_i \right\|_2^2, \tag{1}$$

In the fully connected autoencoder,

$$\begin{aligned} f_W(x) &= \sigma(Wx) \equiv h \\ g_U(h) &= \sigma(Uh) \end{aligned} \tag{2}$$

where x and h are vectors, W is the learn weights, and σ is the activation function. After learning, the embedded vector h is a unique representation for input. In our application, the convolutional autoencoders (CAE) are defined as

$$\begin{aligned} f_W(x) &= \sigma(x * W) \equiv h \\ g_U(h) &= \sigma(h * U) \end{aligned} \tag{3}$$

where x and h are the matrix or tensor and "*" is the convolutional operator.

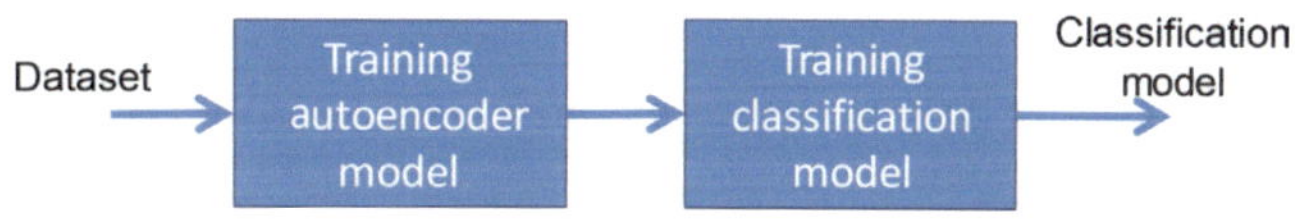

Figure 1.
Flowchart of the method.

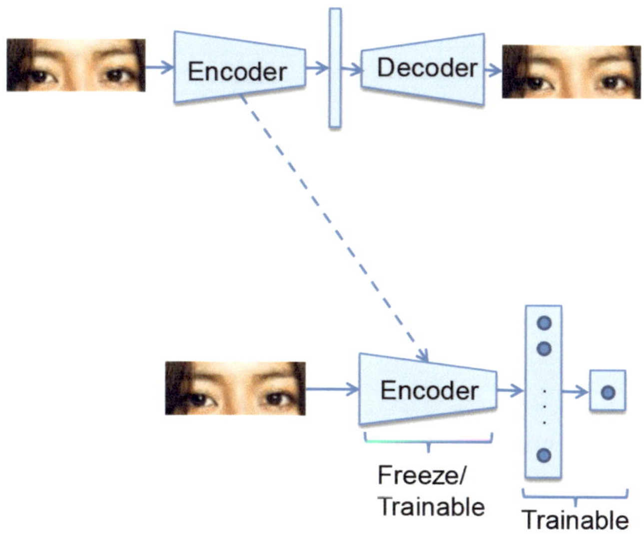

Figure 2.
Method of training the feature extractor.

We propose the CAE-based feature extraction method that learns the generic feature of the face. The encoder serves as the feature extractor that encodes the image into vector h that represent the image of the facial part, for example, the eyes.

In **Table 1**, the several model structures that we use in our experiment were shown. We tried four models. The differences between the four models are the number of layers and dimension of the embedded vector. The number of layers in autoencoders vary between 3 and 4 layers, while the dimensions of the embedded vector are 32 and 64.

3.2 Perfection prediction system

After training the autoencoder, it will serve as the feature extractor as shown in **Figure 2**. In this step, we apply the transfer learning method to transfer the well-learned filters for facial part feature extraction. We try two different lengths of the embedding vector, say, 32 and 64, as shown in **Table 1**. We also try both to freeze and to retrain the extractor.

This model predicts the probability of perfection; the output range of the model is a one-dimensional vector with the interval of [0–1] that reflects the probability of perfection. The probability of perfection is defined as follows:

- If the face is perfect (no surgery is needed), the probability is 1.
- If the face is not perfect (surgery is needed to be performed), the probability is 0.

However, in a real situation, we cannot obtain a big dataset of the perfect/non-perfect face. Thus, we assume that the outcome of surgery is perfect (value is 1) and the original face is not perfect (value is 0).

3 layers											
Autoencoder 1		**Layer**	**#kernel**	**kernel size**	**stride**	**input size**			**output size**		
	Encoder	conv*	32	5*5	2*2	256	80	3	64	20	32
		conv*	32	3*3	1*1	64	20	32	32	10	32
		conv	64	3*3	1*1	32	10	32	32	10	64
	Decoder	deconv*	32	3*3	1*1	32	10	64	64	20	32
		deconv*	32	3*3	1*1	64	20	32	128	40	32
		deconv	3	5*5	2*2	128	40	32	256	80	3
Model classifier 1		**Layer**	**output**								
		Encoder									
		Dense	64								
		Dense	1								
Autoencoder 2		**Layer**	**#kernel**	**kernel size**	**stride**	**input size**			**output size**		
	Encoder	conv*	16	5*5	2*2	256	80	3	64	20	16
		conv*	16	3*3	1*1	64	20	16	32	10	16
		conv	32	3*3	1*1	32	10	16	32	10	32
	Decoder	deconv*	16	3*3	1*1	32	10	32	64	20	16
		deconv*	16	3*3	1*1	64	20	16	128	40	16
		deconv	3	5*5	2*2	128	40	16	256	80	3
Model classifier 2		**Layer**	**output**								
		Encoder									
		Dense	32								
		Dense	1								
4 layers											
Autoencoder 3		**Layer**	**#kernel**	**kernel size**	**stride**	**input size**			**output size**		
	Encoder	conv*	32	5*5	2*2	256	80	3	64	20	32
		conv*	32	3*3	1*1	64	20	32	32	10	32
		conv*	64	3*3	1*1	32	10	32	16	5	64
		conv	64	3*3	1*1	16	5	64	16	5	64
	Decoder	deconv*	64	3*3	1*1	16	5	64	32	10	64
		deconv*	32	3*3	1*1	32	10	64	64	20	32
		deconv*	32	3*3	1*1	64	20	32	128	40	32
		deconv	3	5*5	2*2	128	40	32	256	80	3
Model classifier 3		**Layer**	**output**								
		Encoder									
		Dense	64								
		Dense	1								
Autoencoder 4		**Layer**	**#kernel**	**kernel size**	**stride**	**input size**			**output size**		
	Encoder	conv*	16	5*5	2*2	256	80	3	64	20	16
		conv*	16	3*3	1*1	64	20	16	32	10	16
		conv*	32	3*3	1*1	32	10	16	16	5	32
		conv	32	3*3	1*1	16	5	32	16	5	32
	Decoder	deconv*	32	3*3	1*1	16	5	32	32	10	32
		deconv*	16	3*3	1*1	32	10	32	64	20	16
		deconv*	16	3*3	1*1	64	20	16	128	40	16
		deconv	3	5*5	2*2	128	40	16	256	80	3
Model classifier 4		**Layer**	**output**								
		Encoder									
		Dense	32								
		Dense	1								

conv: convolution. conv: convolution and max-pooling with filter size (2.2). deconv: transposed convolution. deconv*: (2.2) upsampling with transposed convolution.*

Table 1.
Autoencoder model and classification model.

4. Experiment

4.1 Dataset preparation

In the dataset, the total number of images of rejuvenation treatment and eye double-fold surgery are 5585 and 36,598 pairs of the images, respectively. The data is filtered to select a good image for training. Some errors in the images are not well aligned, only one eye, etc. The reject rates are 82.15 and 59.92%, respectively.

The image was crop around the eye area. Then the data is divided into 70, 15, and 15% for training, validation, and testing, respectively.

As mentioned earlier, the output of the model is the probability of perfection. Hence, our training data include the image of before and after surgery as shown in **Figure 3**.

4.2 Prediction accuracy

We chose a thresholding value for the prediction model. If the predicted value is higher than the thresholding value, the face is predicted to be perfect. From that, we obtain accuracy of the different models as shown in **Tables 2** and **3**. We have two schemes of training in which the feature extractors are freezed (not training together with the classification model) and trainable, resulting in eight models in these two tables. When the feature extractor is freezed, we believe that it has already captured universal features such as edge and curves which is relevant to our tasks. Therefore, we want to keep the weights of the feature extract intact. However, in the second training scheme, we apply different learning rates for the feature extractor and the fully connected layers. The learning rate of the feature extractor is much smaller than that of the fully connected layer because we believe that the weights of the feature extractor is good enough for our tasks and we do not want to distort them too quickly and too much during the training of the classification model.

These above training schemes are the best common practices when fine-tuning deep neural networks. We tried both of them, resulting in the following. The best model for double-fold surgery and rejuvenation treatment are Models 1 and 8 (see **Tables 2** and **3** for more details), with accuracy on the test dataset of 93.1 and 88.9%, respectively. Model 1 is the model when the encoder

Figure 3.
Example of original and outcome of surgery.

Name	Classifier	Training Method	Result on test-data		Result on validation-data		Filter 1 - accuracy	Filter 2 - loss function
			Loss function	Accuracy	Loss function	Accuracy		
Model 1	Classifier 1	Free encoder	0.200	0.931	0.189	0.938	0.935	0.195
Model 2	Classifier 1	Trainable encoder	0.255	0.923	0.199	0.944	0.934	0.227
Model 3	Classifier 2	Free encoder	0.204	0.924	0.179	0.932	0.928	0.192
Model 4	Classifier 2	Trainable encoder	0.368	0.929	0.318	0.940	0.935	0.343
Model 5	Classifier 3	Free encoder	0.194	0.927	0.165	0.939	0.933	0.180
Model 6	Classifier 3	Trainable encoder	0.354	0.939	0.275	0.950	0.945	0.315
Model 7	Classifier 4	Free encoder	0.192	0.925	0.172	0.935	0.930	0.182
Model 8	Classifier 4	Trainable encoder	0.219	0.928	0.173	0.948	0.938	0.196

Table 2.
Testing accuracy for eye double-fold surgery.

Name	Classifier	Training Method	Result on test-data		Result on validation-data		Filter 1 - accuracy	Filter 2 - loss function
			Loss function	Accuracy	Loss function	Accuracy		
Model 1	Classifier 1	Free encoder	0.506	0.885	0.859	0.854	0.870	0.083
Model 2	Classifier 1	Trainable encoder	0.938	0.861	0.782	0.902	0.882	0.860
Model 3	Classifier 2	Free encoder	0.370	0.857	0.469	0.844	0.851	0.420
Model 4	Classifier 2	Trainable encoder	0.783	0.895	0.969	0.885	0.890	0.876
Model 5	Classifier 3	Free encoder	0.328	0.854	0.410	0.868	0.861	0.369
Model 6	Classifier 3	Trainable encoder	0.618	0.892	0.594	0.906	0.899	0.606
Model 7	Classifier 4	Free encoder	0.362	0.861	0.542	0.861	0.861	0.452
Model 8	Classifier 4	Trainable encoder	0.662	0.889	0.512	0.923	0.906	0.587

Table 3.
Testing accuracy for rejuvenation treatment.

was freezed. However, in Model 8, the encoder was retrained. However, the accuracy differences between the best model and the second best model are less than 1%.

5. Conclusion

We have presented in this chapter an interesting application of deep learning in aesthetic surgery recommendation along with its encouraging results. By using our system, the presented deep learning engine will provide a reference decision of taking either rejuvenation treatment or eye double-fold surgery or not to both the surgeon and the patient, just based on the eye photo of the patient. To this end, we trained a deep autoencoder by our in-house dataset, composing of pairs of images captured before and after the surgery. The trained encoder part learned in an unsupervised manner, a rich set of features, characterized both unattractive and beautiful facial features. We concatenate the trained encoder part to a fully connected layer to predict perfection score of an eye photo of a patient, based on which a decision of taking treatment or not will be made.

Even though our preliminary results are promising with 88.9 and 93.1% accuracy on rejuvenation treatment and eye double-fold surgery, respectively, it still has much rooms for improvement. Firstly, we should improve the dimension of our in-house dataset by encouraging more patients to participate in our program, so that we are able to build a deeper network. More and more layers are added; richer and richer learned features are obtained to improve the accuracy of our system. Secondly, we are going to expand the capability of our system to deal with more kinds of treatments to diversify and provide the best services to our clients, rather than focusing on the two above treatment and surgery.

Author details

Phan Chau Phuc Thinh[1], Bui Thi Xuyen[1], Nguyen Do Trung Chanh[1], Dao Huu Hung[1*] and Mimura Daisuke[2]

1 Data Science Laboratory, FPT Software Japan Co. Ltd., Tokyo, Japan

2 Shonan Beauty Clinic, Tokyo, Japan

*Address all correspondence to: hungdh3@fsoft.com.vn

References

[1] Alex K, Ilya S, Geoffrey EH. ImageNet classification with deep convolutional neural networks. In: Advances in Neural Information Processing Systems. 2012

[2] Christian S, Wei L, Yangqing J, Pierre S, Scott R, Dragomir A, et al. Going deeper with convolutions. In: Computer Vision and Pattern Recognition. 2014

[3] Karen S, Andrew Z. Very deep convolutional networks for large-scale image recognition. In: Computer Vision and Pattern Recognition. 2014

[4] Kaiming H, Xiangyu Z, Shaoqing R, Jian S. Deep residual learning for image recognition. In: IEEE Conference on Computer Vision and Pattern Recognition. 2015

[5] Naiyan W, Dit-Yan Y. Learning a deep compact image representation for visual tracking. In: Advances in Neural Information Processing Systems. 2013

[6] Florian S, Dmitry K, James P. FaceNet: A unified embedding for face recognition and clustering. In: IEEE Conference on Computer Vision and Pattern Recognition. 2015

[7] Joseph R, Santosh D, Ross G, Ali F. You only look once: Unified, real-time object detection. In: IEEE Conference on Computer Vision and Pattern Recognition. 2016

[8] Bahram L, Mehdi FS, Ihsan U. Survey on deep learning techniques for person re-identification task. In: IEEE Conference on Computer Vision and Pattern Recognition. 2018

[9] Richa S, Mayank V, Afzel N. Effects of plastic surgery on face recognition: A preliminary study. In: IEEE Conference on Computer Vision and Pattern Recognition; Minami. 2009

[10] Amal SOA, Vijanth S, Aamir M, Azrina A. Proposed face recognition system after plastic surgery. IET Computer Vision. 2016;**10**(5):344-350

[11] Maria DM, Michele N, Daniel R, Harry W. Robust face recognition after plastic surgery using region-based approaches. Pattern Recognition. 2015;**48**(4):1261-1276

[12] De Marsico M, Nappi M, Riccio D. FARO: Face recognition against occlusions and expression variations. IEEE Transactions on Systems, Man, and Cybernetics, Part A Systems and Humans. 2010;**40**(1):121-132

[13] De Marsico M, Nappi M, Riccio D. FACE: Face analysis for commercial entities. In: IEEE International Conference on Image Processing; Hong Kong. 2010

[14] Michele N, Stefano R, Massimo T. When plastic surgery challenges face recognition. Image and Vision Computing. 2016;**54**:71-82

[15] Sanzhar A, Yujin A, Jiho B, Andrey V, Gil-Jin J, Pilun K, et al. Quantitative classification of OCT skin images with deep learning. In: Proceedings SPIE 10467, Photonics in Dermatology and Plastic Surgery. 2018

[16] Alarifi JS, Goyal M, Davison A, Dancey D, Khan R, Yap M. Facial skin classification using convolutional neural networks. In: Image Analysis and Recognition ICIAR. 2017

[17] Nazre B, Rama C. Modeling of facial wrinkles for applications in computer vision. In: Advances in Face Detection and Facial Image Analysis. Springer; 2016. pp. 299-332. https://www.springerprofessional.de/en/modeling-of-facial-wrinkles-for-applications-in-computer-vision/9975942

[18] Yikui Z, He C, Wenbo D, Junying G, Vincenzo P, Junying Z. BeautyNet: Joint multiscale CNN and transfer learning method for unconstrained facial beauty prediction. Computational Intelligence and Neuroscience. 2019;**2019**:1-14

[19] Lu X, Jinhai X, Xiaohui Y. Transferring rich deep features for facial beauty prediction. 2018. pp. 1-6. arXiv:1803.07253 [cs.CV]

[20] Arakawa K, Nomoto K. A system for beautifying face images using interactive evolutionary computing. In: International Symposium on Intelligent Signal Processing and Communication Systems. 2005

[21] Tommer L, Daniel C-O, Gideon D, Dani L. Data-driven enhancement of facial attractiveness. In: Proceeding ACM Siggraph. 2008

[22] Bottino A, Laurentini A, Rosano L. A new computer-aided technique for planning the aesthetic outcome of plastic surgery. In: International Conference in Central Europe on Computer Graphics, Visualization and Computer Vision, Plzen—Bory. 2008

[23] Guo X, Liu X, Zhu E, Yin J. Deep clustering with convolutional autoencoders. In: International Conference on Neural Information Processing. 2017

Chapter 5

An Assessment of the Prediction Quality of VPIN

Antoine Bambade and Kesheng Wu

Abstract

VPIN is a tool designed to predict extreme events like flash crashes. Some concerns have been raised about its reliability. In this chapter we assess VPIN prediction quality (precision and recall rates) of extreme volatility events including its sensitivity to the starting point of computation in a given data set. We benchmark the results with the ones of a "naive classifier." The test data used in this study contains 5.6 year's worth of trading data of the five most liquid futures contracts of this time period. We found that VPIN has poor "flash crash" prediction power with the traditional 0.99 decision threshold. Increasing the decision threshold does not significantly improve overall prediction quality. Nevertheless we found VPIN has a more interesting predictive power for flash events of lower amplitude. Finally, we found that, for practice, the last bar price structure is the least sensitive to the starting point of computation.

Keywords: high-frequency data, probability of informed trading, VPIN, liquidity, flow toxicity, volume imbalance, flash crash
JEL codes: C02, D52, D53, G14, G23

1. Introduction

1.1 Main study purpose

Easley et al. [1] designed a tool, nicknamed volume-synchronized probability of informed trading (VPIN), with the aim to predict flash crashes. It appeared it could predict the "flash crash" of May 6, 2010, a few hours before it happened [2]. A lot of papers were published [3–5], and it was proposed to use it for regulation through a VPIN contract [2, 6]. However, critics pointed out some flaws, questioning its reliability [7–11] but without providing a quantitative evaluation of the prediction quality (e.g., in terms of precision and recall rates). In this study, we design a framework to detect flash crashes and thereby assess the behavior of the VPIN tool enabling as well as comparing and benchmarking with other predictive algorithms.

1.2 Motivation

The amount of trading data has exploded in finance thanks to the continuing progress of high-frequency techniques. It constrains practitioners to use more and more state-of-the-art algorithms to deal with this overwhelming amount of information. Computers and algorithms are more and more efficient, but still decision-making is highly dependent on both the quantity and the quality of information. Thus, errors and speculations that can make the financial market toxic, i.e., conducive to crashes, are possible. Examples in the past, such as the "flash crash" of May 6, 2010, have shown that this new paradigm in finance has made it possible to introduce a new kind of crashes characterized by their suddenness. Such quick crashes seem dangerous because of a kind of inherent unpredictability. However, predictive models to model this new framework do exist.

1.3 Model

Easley et al. [12] designed a model of the high-frequency financial market based on flows of informed and uninformed traders. They showed that information is a key parameter of the spread between ask and bid of prices. The model works as follows. Each day, general conditions and circumstances may or may not result in events that can help predict the evolution of the price of a future. More precisely, for each day, nature decides whether or not there is an event that can help predict the evolution of the price of a future. This is modeled with a Bernoulli law of parameter α. If an event occurs, nature also decides with a Bernoulli law of parameter δ if this event is a low signal. With these conditions, buys and sells for this future come then from flows of informed and uninformed traders. They are modeled by Poisson processes of respective parameters μ and ϵ. This framework can be summarized by the following tree in **Figure 1** [13].

The whole trading process studied is thus a mixture of Poisson processes. It enabled authors to compute ask and bid and then the spread. They showed that for reasonable cases the spread is linearly linked with the following probability they named probability of informed trading (PIN) [12]:

$$PIN = \frac{\alpha\mu}{\alpha\mu + 2\epsilon}. \tag{1}$$

Later, Easley et al. [2] designed a new framework to easily compute this probability. Indeed PIN numbers come from a parametrized framework, and one does not have access to all these parameters. They showed however that PIN can be well approximated through a volume-clock paradigm [14], thanks to data of futures

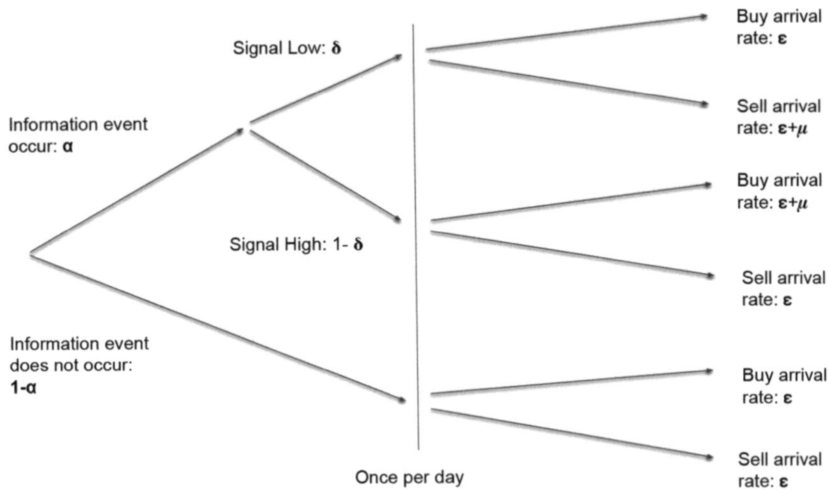

Figure 1.
A tree summarizing the trading process.

with a new formula. The approximated version of PIN was then called the volume-synchronized probability of informed trading (VPIN). It appeared that this new tool could predict the "flash crash" of May 6, 2010, a few hours before it happened [2].

Nevertheless, the model has received a lot of critics. For example, Andersen and Bondarenko have shown [7] that VPIN is quite sensitive to the starting point of when one starts computing VPIN on a data set. It indeed questions VPIN prediction quality. Moreover, they have also shown that VPIN is sensitive to other parameters, such as the trade classification rule used [8] or how one defines the average daily volume of trades [9]. Changing the classification rule may drastically change VPIN behavior [9]. Pöppe et al. have reached the same conclusions with a different approach. Using a different classification rule can change VPIN prediction power toward a crash (in their paper a German blue-chip stock [11]). Besides, controlling ex ante parameters seems to give poorer prediction quality [8, 9]. This point has also been checked by Abad et al. [10]. Controlling ex ante realized volatility, and trading intensity, as did Andersen and Bondarenko [9], prediction quality seems to vanish. More deeply, they have also underlined that it is not obvious how one should define a VPIN prediction, analyzing more precisely toxic and nontoxic halts, as well as toxic events. Furthermore, Torben G. Andersen and Oleg Bondarenko interpret VPIN as being too sensitive to trading intensity. They have also explained that VPIN metric is sometimes unexpectedly correlated with other usual ones (such as VIX or RV) [7, 8]. More recently, it has been shown theoretically that the volume-clock paradigm of VPIN framework does not enable to really approximate fully the PIN value, although the proposed formula is close [15, 16].

More generally, all these critics have pointed out that:

- First, it is not obvious how one should use VPIN.
- Second, prediction quality has not been studied sufficiently to assess it as being reliable.
- Third, the study lacks objective benchmark.

1.4 Goal

The purpose of this chapter is to quantify the prediction quality of VPIN in order to enable practitioners to assess whether or not it can be used in the real world (e.g., for trading or regulation). That's why:

- First, we want to design a proper framework to compute precision and recall rates as well as prediction length of VPIN. This will be possible by providing a formal definition of flash crashes. To be more precise, we will use the maximum of intermediate return (MIR) [5] to define it.
- Second, we want to study through this framework how sensitive VPIN is to the starting point of the data set.

1.5 Plan

In the following, we first recall VPIN model and propose a definition for flash crashes (Section 2). Second, we assess within this framework VPIN prediction quality (Section 3). Finally, we assess VPIN sensitivity to the starting point of the data set (Section 4).

2. VPIN software and formal flash crash definition

In this section, we first recall the VPIN model. Second, we propose a definition of flash crashes used to compute precision and recall rates. Finally, we present the data used in our tests.

2.1 VPIN software

Easley et al. [12] designed a model of the high-frequency financial market based on informed and uninformed traders. It is then possible to compute a probability of informed trading (PIN). Easley et al. [1] use these results and define an easy way to compute PIN only through the data of trades. We describe briefly VPIN model used in previous literature. The theoretic study of the model is treated in another research study.

2.1.1 Bars

Following Easley et al. [1], a bar is a fixed volume of trades that are successive in time. With such a definition, one can associate the following quantities with each bar:

- A nominal price, computed according to a given technique (mean price, median price, closing price, opening price, etc.)
- A nominal time (first trade time, last trade time)
- Local maximum and minimum values of trades

In practice, the last few trades that do not fill up a bar are dropped to the next bar.

2.1.2 Bulk volume classification

The computation of VPIN requires to determine directions of trades, i.e., classifying each trade as a buy or a sell. The method used here is the following: bulk volume classification (BVC) [1, 5]. Let us note V_b the volume of a bar and j the label of bar number j (j>0) and P_j its price (closing, opening, median, mean). Then the number of buys V_j^b within bar j is determined according to this formula:

$$V_j^b = V_b \mathcal{Z}\left(\frac{P_j - P_{j-1}}{\sigma}\right) \tag{2}$$

where $\mathcal{Z}$ is the cumulative function of a given law (usually student or normal distribution) and σ is the standard deviation of the numerator on successive number of bars. In our test, σ is computed once on all successive values of the data set, and the student law is of parameter one. Within bar j the number of sells V_j^s is obviously

$$V_j^s = V_b\left(1 - \mathcal{Z}\left(\frac{P_j - P_{j-1}}{\sigma}\right)\right) \tag{3}$$

2.1.3 Buckets

A bucket is defined to be a fixed number of successive trades. Here to simplify, as bars are defined also as a fixed number of trades, a bucket will be m successive bars. Let us note V_{bucket} the fixed volume of a bucket. We naturally have $V_{bucket} = mV_b$.

2.1.4 VPIN formula

VPIN formula is computed on n successive buckets, where n is VPIN support. A buffer is defined as n successive buckets. Here is VPIN formula, approximating (1) upon bucket number j ($j \geq n$):

$$VPIN_j = \frac{\sum_{i=j-n+1}^{j} |V^b_{bucket,\,i} - V^s_{bucket,\,i}|}{nV_{bucket}} \tag{4}$$

For a given bucket i:

- $V^s_{bucket,\,i} = \sum_{j \in bucket_i} V^s_j$
- $V^b_{bucket,\,i} = \sum_{j \in bucket_i} V^b_j$

In order to distribute all VPIN values between 0 and 1, in practice, VPIN is normalized through a normal law. We thus consider $VPIN_{normalized}$ in the following:

2.1.5 VPIN event

A VPIN event is declared when the following occurs:

$$VPIN_{normalized} \geq \theta_{VPIN} \tag{5}$$

where θ_{VPIN} is a given decision threshold. In practice [5] $\theta_{VPIN} = 0.99$.

2.2 Defining flash crashes with MIR

2.2.1 Formal definition

Let $(p_t)_t$ be a time series (e.g., of prices). Here is the definition of MIR:

$$MIR_{t,\,\eta} = max_{i \neq j,\, i,j \in [t,t+\eta]} \frac{|p_i - p_j|}{p_i} \tag{6}$$

A flash crash will depend on two things here:

- The amplitude of the crash, which means extreme MIR values (e.g., 10%)
- The shortness of the fall, which means the shortness of the time window within η that computes $MIR_{t,\,\eta}$ (e.g., 10 minutes), more precisely, noting $i^*, j^* = argmax_{i \neq j,\, i,j \in [t,t+\eta]} \frac{|p_i - p_j|}{p_i}$, the fall has length $|j^* - i^*|$

2.2.2 Empiric definition

We reported in this data set only one flash crash, i.e., on May 6, 2010, which lasted approximately 10 minutes according to media and financial institutions. Our definition of flash crash will obviously take into account this event.

2.3 The data

2.3.1 Futures used

In this work, we use a comprehensive set of liquid futures trading data to illustrate the techniques to be introduced. More specifically, we will use 67 months' worth of tick data of the five most liquid futures traded on all asset classes. The data comes to us in the form of 5 CSV files, one for each futures contract traded. The source of our data is TickWrite, a data vendor that normalizes the data into a common structure after acquiring it directly from the relevant exchanges. The total size of the comma-separated value (CSV) files is about 45.1 GB. They contain about millions of trades spanning from the beginning of January 2007 to the end of July 2012. The data set contains five of the most heavily traded futures contracts. Each has more than 100 million trades during this 67-month period. The most heavily traded futures, the file containing E-mini SP500 futures, symbol ES, has about 500 million trades involving a total number of about 3 billion contracts. The second most heavily traded futures is Euro exchange rates, symbol EC, which is 188 million trades. The next three are Nasdaq 100 (NQ), 173 million trades; light crude oil (CL), 165 million trades; and E-mini Dow Jones (YM), 110 million trades. In **Figure 2**, one can see an evolution of prices with time (here each tick corresponds to a bucket).

2.3.2 Definition of flash crash

We want to define empirically a flash crash using the tools of VPIN framework, namely, bars and buckets. As volume-clock paradigm does not allow to control filling times of fixed volume of trades, here below is a summary of the steps we have followed to manage to detect flash crashes using MIR. As it is quite long and the main purpose of study is the prediction of results of the following section, we present principles and do not go into technical details:

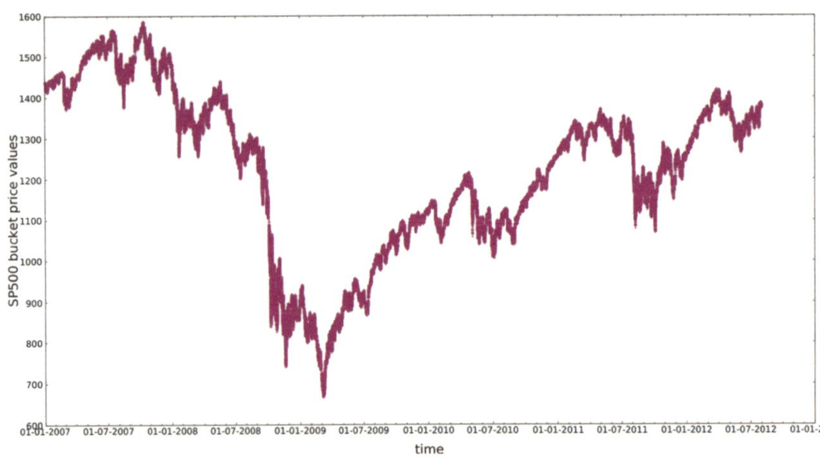

Figure 2.
Bucket S&P 500 values with time.

- To be sure not to miss a flash crash because of being too long in time bar or bucket, we have chosen a reasonable granularity level as in [5] (buckets per day, 200, and bars per bucket, 30).

- For each financial instrument, we have recorded the number of bars necessary to capture the local 10 minutes of maximum fall of May 6, 2010, known as the "flash crash"; we refer to these numbers as "window lengths" below.

- As the window lengths defined above do not have a stable distribution in time (because of the volume-clock paradigm), we have arbitrarily filtered out all events in which the time difference between minimum and maximum within a window length is longer than 20 minutes, in order to capture only quick events. Indeed, one given window length may be too big and thus allow at some date to measure a time difference between local minimum and maximum which is longer than 10 minutes whereas it would be a true flash crash with a smaller window length.[1]

- For each instrument we recorded the amplitude of the "flash crash" and their respective MIR values.

The results made it possible to classify the five financial instruments into two groups:

- Data sets where the "flash crash" and other flash crashes are significantly present: ES, NQ, and YM.

- Data sets where the "flash crash" and other flash crashes are not really present. More precisely, the "flash crash" is not a rare event in the data set, and generally magnitude levels of flash crashes are low compared to other instruments.

3. Assessing VPIN prediction quality

In this section, first we present our methodology to find VPIN optimal prediction quality (for which recall and precision rates are maximal and more useful for practice). Second, we present all the results: best parameters, associated remarks, and prediction lengths.

3.1 Methodology

3.1.1 Parameters to test

Here are the parameters we will test:

[1] This is not perfect because we can still miss some crashes (whereas in this data set, it will not be that much, and it will be with a smaller probability), but first we do not want to change too much the definition in time of a flash crash (we will not increase the tolerance level to 1 day), and second this problem is inherent to the fact that fixing volume of bars and of buckets prevents us from controlling precisely filling bar and bucket times. Finding a solution for this precise data set does not guarantee at all a general solution neither for one data set nor for a financial instrument.

- Bar price: mean, median, last price, first price
- MIR decision threshold θ_{MIR} to detect a flash crash
- VPIN support n
- VPIN classifier (student, normal)
- Prediction window ω (described below)
- VPIN decision threshold θ_{VPIN} to predict a flash crash

3.1.2 Defining true positive events

Here we describe how we define true positive, false-negative, and false-positive events. For a given prediction window length ω:

- From a MIR flash crash detection (i.e., $MIR_j \geq \theta_{MIR}$) at a bucket j ($j \geq \omega$), if in the window of buckets [j-ω,j-1] there is a VPIN event (i.e., $VPIN_{Normalized,i} \geq \theta_{VPIN}$, i ∈ [j-$\omega$,j-1]), then we consider it as a true positive event.[2] Otherwise it is a false-negative event.

- From a VPIN event at a bucket j (i.e., $VPIN_{Normalized,j} \geq \theta_{VPIN}$, $j+\omega \leq end\ Of\ DataSet$), if in the window of buckets [j + 1,j + ω] there is a flash crash ((i.e., $MIR_i \geq \theta_{MIR}$, i ∈ [j+1,j+ω]), then we consider it as a true positive event.[3] Otherwise it is a false-positive event.

3.1.3 Choosing the maximum value of ω

To make a useful deep search, we have computed the distribution of time difference between different amounts ω of buckets. Indeed, we want to control a temporal time window reasonable for practitioners and still sufficiently wide so that we can analyze which events VPIN can detect or not. We have focused this research to have a stable bounded distribution of time difference between ω buckets of about 1 month. Below one can see the respective distribution for the *S&P*500 instrument; the four other distributions of the instruments studied look the same (**Figure 3**).

In **Table 1** one can see the medians of the different distributions.

For the next step, $\omega \leq 2500$.

3.1.4 Describing deep search of flash crash prediction

Here we describe how we intend to make a first deep search of VPIN prediction quality of events close to the "Flash Crash" of May 2010. In this algorithm described below θ_{VPIN} = 0.99.[4]

For each VPIN classifier (student or Gaussian), for each bar price structure (last, first, median, average) do:

- For each $\theta_{MIR} \in [5.2\%, 6.2\%]$ with step 0.1% for ES instrument, $\theta_{MIR} \in [2.2\%, 3.2\%]$ with step 0.1% for CL instrument, $\theta_{MIR} \in [0.4\%, 0.9\%]$ with

---

[2] If $j-\omega < 0$, the window of buckets considered is [0,j-1].

[3] If $j+\omega > endOfDataSet$, the window of buckets considered is [j + 1,endOfDataSet].

[4] Previous research, such as [5], showed that this threshold is a good one.

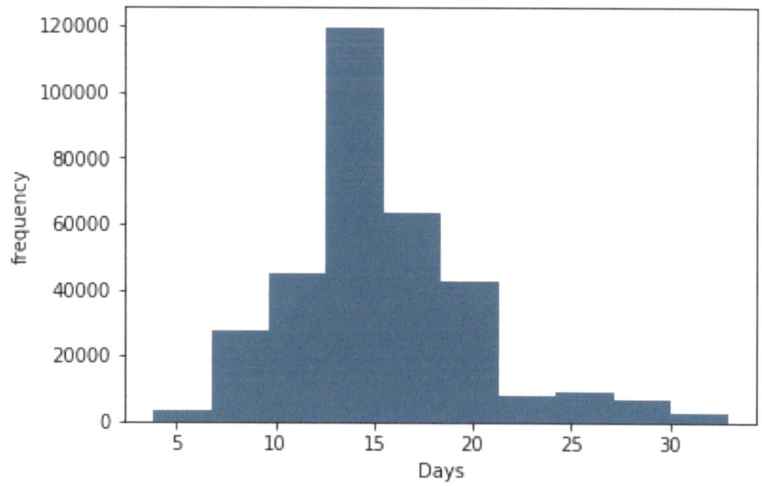

Figure 3.
Time difference distribution between 2500 S&P 500 buckets.

Futures	Days	Number of bucket chosen
ES	14.8	2500
EC	13.8	2500
CL	15.0	2500
YM	14.3	2500
NQ	15.2	2500

Table 1.
Median of time difference between 2500 buckets for the different instruments.

step 0.1% for EC instrument, $\theta_{MIR} \in [8\%, 9\%]$ with step 0.1% for NQ instrument, $\theta_{MIR} \in [5.4\%, 6.4\%]$ with step 0.1% for YM instrument[5] do:

- For each VPIN support $n \in [30, 60]$, with step 10, do:
    - For $\omega \in [100, 2500]$ with step 100, do:
    - test prediction
    - store current parameters, precision and recall if and only if $recall + precision \geq previousLocalMaximum$
    - store prediction length (distance between VPIN event and MIR event).

Remark. we first try to maximize precision+recall rate. If the local maximum found is interesting for practice (at least superior or equal to 1.2) and more powerful than a "naive" algorithm, then it sounds worth making a more serious search of precision and recall rates separately to find a good trade-off between them (e.g., thanks to a ROC curve).

[5] As each MIR value for the flash crash is different, one must adapt the area of deep search to be precise and have a quicker calculation time.

3.2 Results

3.2.1 Best parameters found

In **Tables 2–5** one case see the best parameters that maximize precision+recall for each financial instrument and bar price structure studied.

3.2.2 Remarks and first interpretation

We remark overall the following:

- The choice of bar structure does not really affect the optimal choice of other parameters; nevertheless mean and median bar price structures have best precision+recall rate on average.
- Recall rates are very close to 1.
- Since ES, NQ, and YM precision rates are "low", thus precision + recall rates are "low."
- Since EC and CL precision rates are "high," thus precision + recall rates are "high" since recall is already "high."
- CL and EC had on May 6, 2010, a very low flash crash threshold, which increases a lot the number of crash of same magnitude detected in the data set.
- CL and EC obtain their maximum value to the minimum bound of the deep search (respectively, a 2.2% fall and 0.6% fall). It is not the case for other

Futures	Recall	Precision	Precision+recall	θ_{MIR}	n	ω (buckets)	Classifier	Bar price
ES	0.9737	0.2171	1.1908	0.062	60	2400	Gaussian	Last
EC	0.9080	0.9644	1.8724	0.006	30	2500	Gaussian	Last
CL	0.9406	0.9045	1.8451	0.022	60	2500	Student	Last
NQ	1	0.0034	1.0034	0.08	30	400	Gaussian	Last
YM	0.8421	0.1512	0.9933	0.064	60	2500	Gaussian	Last

Table 2.
Best parameters maximizing precision+recall rate for different futures and last bar price structure in the first deep search.

Futures	Recall	Precision	Precision+recall	θ_{MIR}	n	ω (buckets)	Classifier	Bar price
ES	0.9737	0.2024	1.1761	0.062	60	2400	Gaussian	First
EC	0.9127	0.9681	1.8808	0.006	30	2500	Student	First
CL	0.9534	0.9012	1.8546	0.022	60	2500	Student	First
NQ	1	0.0038	1.0038	0.08	30	400	Gaussian	First
YM	0.8421	0.1449	0.9870	0.064	60	2500	Gaussian	First

Table 3.
Best parameters maximizing precision+recall rate for different futures and first bar price structure in the first deep search.

Futures	Recall	Precision	Precision+recall	θ_{MIR}	n	ω (buckets)	Classifier	Bar price
ES	0.9737	0.1996	1.1733	0.062	60	2400	Gaussian	Median
EC	0.9037	0.9718	1.8755	0.006	30	2500	Student	Median
CL	0.9447	0.8951	1.8398	0.022	60	2500	Student	Median
NQ	1	0.0036	1.0036	0.08	30	400	Gaussian	Median
YM	1	0.1911	1.1911	0.054	30	2500	Student	Median

Table 4.
Best parameters maximizing precision+recall rate for different futures and median bar price structure in the first deep search.

Futures	Recall	Precision	Precision+recall	θ_{MIR}	n	ω (buckets)	Classifier	Bar price
ES	0.9737	0.1950	1.1687	0.062	60	2400	Student	Mean
EC	0.9058	0.9691	1.8749	0.006	30	2500	Student	Mean
CL	0.9789	0.8654	1.8443	0.022	40	2500	Student	Mean
NQ	1	0.0036	1.0036	0.08	30	400	Gaussian	Mean
YM	1	0.1921	1.1921	0.055	30	2500	Student	Mean

Table 5.
Best parameters maximizing precision+recall rate for different futures and mean bar price structure in the first deep search.

instruments (in NQ cases, precision+recall optimal rate is constant from 0.8 to 0.9).

The results give two first findings:

- When the flash crash is significantly present for the instrument, i.e., of high magnitude and rare in the data set (ES, YM, and NQ cases), then recall is high, which means that VPIN makes a prediction before this happens, but precision is low: VPIN detects other events that are not flash crashes.
- When the flash crash is not significantly present for the instrument, i.e., of low magnitude and not rare (there are a lot of events of 10–20-minute length of same magnitude), then recall and precision are high.

This may suggest one of the following hypotheses:

- VPIN seems to be a poor indicator of flash crash prediction with the usual recommended threshold 0.99.
- VPIN can be a better indicator of another type of event (crashes of less important amplitude).

We will compare the results of the same deep search with the one of a naive classifier, to see whether or not the good prediction results in CL and ES cases are relevant.

3.2.3 Benchmark with a "naive classifier"

We made a comparison of VPIN prediction quality result with a "naive classifier," which randomly chooses whether or not there will be a crash from each

Futures	Recall	Precision	Precision+recall	θ_{MIR}	n	ω (buckets)
ES	1	0.0355	1.0355	0.052	50	2500
EC	1	0.9948	1.9948	0.004	50	2500
CL	1	0.3413	1.3413	0.022	50	2500
NQ	1	0.0076	1.0076	0.084	60	2500
YM	1	0.0174	1.0174	0.055	50	2500

Table 6.
Best parameters maximizing precision+recall rate for different futures for the naive classifier.

bucket of the data set. In **Table 6** one can see the results of the naive classifier for the first deep search set of parameters.[6] As it is a naive classifier, results do not depend on direction of prices (bar price classifier) and bar price structure.

We remark the following:

- "Naive classifier" has poor results comparable to those of VPIN for ES, NQ, and YM instruments; although poor, VPIN predictions are better than "naive algorithm" on ES cases.
- "Naive classifier" has better results than VPIN on EC instrument.
- "Naive classifier" has worse results than VPIN on CL instrument.

We can interpret it as follows:

- EC flash crash definition is barely inconsistent, with a MIR threshold of 0.006%; it is obvious that a naive algorithm does better results as the constraint is very small to detect a "flash crash" of such a magnitude.
- On CL and ES cases though, VPIN predictions are better, and these results are obtained when θ_{MIR} threshold was on the lower bound of the deep search. It might indicate that VPIN software has a better predictive power than a "naive algorithm" not on a "flash crash" amplitude basis but on a lower amplitude level. Nevertheless, one may wonder whether or not this level of amplitude is useful for practitioners.

Anyway, previous results may conclude that for "flash crash" prediction, VPIN has overall equivalent poor power prediction with the traditional threshold $\theta_{VPIN} = 0.99$, as a "naive" algorithm.

That's why in the next paragraph, we benchmark predictive power of "naive" and VPIN algorithms:

- First on higher θ_{VPIN} constraints
- Second on lower bounds of crash amplitude θ_{MIR} while $\theta_{VPIN} = 0.99$
- Third on higher θ_{VPIN} constraints and at the same time lower bounds on θ_{MIR}

[6] First tests conducted with EC instrument have been realized with an average to get more robust results. They are really close to the one obtained here with a single realization of randomness.

Indeed, the first hypothesis is that there are too many false VPIN predictions, i.e., false-positive events, as precision rate is too low and recall rate is too high. That's why one may hope that making θ_{VPIN} constraints higher may reduce the number of VPIN "useless" predictions while not reducing too much recall rate.

3.2.4 Deep search allowing higher bounds for θ_{VPIN}

In the following we have looked to higher bounds for θ_{VPIN} from 0.99 to 0.99999. All other parameters of the deep search are the same. Below, one can see the results in **Tables 7–10**. The results for the naive algorithm are indeed the same.

We remark the following:

- Precision rate has increased for each bar price structure for ES instrument, maintaining recall rate constant to θ_{VPIN} = 0.99 case.
- Precision + recall rate has increased for YM instrument only with a last or first bar price structure, but recall decreased a bit compared to θ_{VPIN} = 0.99 case.

Futures	Recall	Precision	Precision+recall	θ_{MIR}	n	ω (buckets)	Classifier	θ_{VPIN}
ES	0.9737	0.4677	1.4414	0.062	60	1600	Gaussian	0.99999
EC	0.9080	0.9644	1.8724	0.006	30	2500	Gaussian	0.99
CL	0.9406	0.9045	1.8451	0.022	60	2500	Student	0.99
NQ	1	0.0034	1.0034	0.08	30	400	Gaussian	0.99
YM	0.7091	0.3160	1.0251	0.054	60	2500	Student	0.9999

Table 7.
Best parameters maximizing precision+recall rate for different futures and last bar price structure allowing higher bounds for θ_{VPIN}.

Futures	Recall	Precision	Precision+recall	θ_{MIR}	n	ω (buckets)	Classifier	θ_{VPIN}
ES	0.9737	0.3412	1.3149	0.062	60	1200	Gaussian	0.99999
EC	0.9127	0.9681	1.8808	0.006	30	2500	Student	0.99
CL	0.9534	0.9012	1.8546	0.022	60	2500	Student	0.99
NQ	1	0.0038	1.0038	0.08	30	2500	Gaussian	0.99
YM	0.7091	0.3545	1.0636	0.054	60	2500	Student	0.9999

Table 8.
Best parameters maximizing precision+recall rate for different futures and first bar price structure allowing higher bounds for θ_{VPIN}.

Futures	Recall	Precision	Precision+recall	θ_{MIR}	n	ω (buckets)	Classifier	θ_{VPIN}
ES	0.9737	0.3306	1.3043	0.062	30	1700	Gaussian	0.99999
EC	0.9037	0.9718	1.8755	0.006	30	2500	Student	0.99
CL	0.9447	0.8951	1.8398	0.022	60	2500	Student	0.99
NQ	1	0.0036	1.0036	0.08	30	400	Gaussian	0.99
YM	1	0.1911	1.1911	0.054	30	2500	Student	0.99

Table 9.
Best parameters maximizing precision+recall rate for different futures and median bar price structure allowing higher bounds for θ_{VPIN}.

- Compared to the "naive" algorithm, VPIN results are effectively better in ES case. In YM case we still find comparable results.
- On average, mean and median bar price structures have the best precision +recall rate.

To verify whether or not we can get at least better results than a naive algorithm in data sets with a real flash crash, we study in the following first the results allowing lower bounds on θ_{MIR} while $\theta_{VPIN} = 0.99$ and second the results allowing lower bounds on θ_{MIR} and higher constraints on θ_{VPIN}. Indeed, the intuition is that on NQ case, the "flash crash" amplitude constraints are far too high to have a good precision rate, because in this case there are too few events detected with MIR algorithm.

3.2.5 Deep search allowing lower bounds for θ_{MIR}

We remark the following in **Tables 11–14**:

- Results have changed for every instrument except the ES one which has kept the same local maximum as in the first deep search.
- Precision is far higher than before, while recall is still high. Therefore, overall precision + recall rates are "high."
- Optimal θ_{MIR} is around 0.015 for ES, CL, NQ, and YM financial instruments, whereas for EC the previous local maximum around 0.006 remains higher.
- On average, median bar price structure has the best precision+recall rate.

Futures	Recall	Precision	Precision+recall	θ_{MIR}	n	ω (buckets)	Classifier	θ_{VPIN}
ES	0.9737	0.3786	1.3523	0.062	60	1600	Gaussian	0.99999
EC	0.9058	0.9691	1.8749	0.006	30	2500	Student	0.99
CL	0.9789	0.8653	1.8442	0.022	40	2500	Student	0.99
NQ	1	0.0036	1.0036	0.08	30	400	Gaussian	0.99
YM	1	0.1921	1.1921	0.055	30	2500	Student	0.99

Table 10.
Best parameters maximizing precision+recall rate for different futures and mean bar price structure allowing higher bounds for θ_{VPIN}.

Futures	Recall	Precision	Precision+recall	θ_{MIR}	n	ω (buckets)	Classifier	Bar price
ES	0.9421	0.9541	1.8962	0.015	30	2500	Student	Last
EC	0.9080	0.9644	1.8724	0.006	30	2500	Gaussian	Last
CL	0.9297	0.9806	1.9103	0.016	30	2500	Student	Last
NQ	0.9179	0.9019	1.8198	0.015	30	2500	Gaussian	Last
YM	0.9460	0.9696	1.9156	0.015	50	2500	Gaussian	Last

Table 11.
Best parameters maximizing precision+recall rate for different futures and last bar price structure allowing higher bounds for θ_{MIR}.

Futures	Recall	Precision	Precision+recall	θ_{MIR}	n	ω (buckets)	Classifier	Bar price
ES	0.9404	0.9402	1.8806	0.015	30	2500	Gaussian	First
EC	0.9127	0.9681	1.8808	0.006	30	2500	Gaussian	First
CL	0.9233	0.9728	1.8961	0.016	30	2500	Student	First
NQ	0.8291	0.9833	1.8124	0.01	30	2500	Student	First
YM	0.9517	0.9673	1.9190	0.015	50	2500	Student	First

Table 12.
Best parameters maximizing precision+recall rate for different futures and first bar price structure allowing higher bounds for θ_{MIR}.

Futures	Recall	Precision	Precision+recall	θ_{MIR}	n	ω (buckets)	Classifier	Bar price
ES	0.9499	0.9498	1.8997	0.015	30	2500	Student	Median
EC	0.9037	0.9717	1.8754	0.006	30	2500	Student	Median
CL	0.9265	0.9718	1.8983	0.016	30	2500	Student	Median
NQ	0.9243	0.9017	1.8260	0.015	30	2500	Gaussian	Median
YM	0.9829	0.9427	1.9256	0.015	30	2500	Gaussian	Median

Table 13.
Best parameters maximizing precision+recall rate for different futures and median bar price structure allowing higher bounds for θ_{MIR}.

Futures	Recall	Precision	Precision+recall	θ_{MIR}	n	ω (buckets)	Classifier	Bar price
ES	0.9526	0.9454	1.8979	0.015	30	2500	Student	Mean
EC	0.9058	0.9691	1.8749	0.006	30	2500	Student	Mean
CL	0.9302	0.9670	1.8972	0.016	30	2500	Gaussian	Mean
NQ	0.9407	0.8796	1.8203	0.02	60	2500	Gaussian	Mean
YM	0.9446	0.9779	1.9225	0.015	60	2500	Student	Mean

Table 14.
Best parameters maximizing precision+recall rate for different futures and mean bar price structure allowing higher bounds for θ_{MIR}.

In the following, we will first compare the results to the case where we allow higher bound on θ_{VPIN}, to see if there is a difference. Second, we will benchmark both results to the one of a "naive" classifier.

3.2.6 Deep search allowing lower bounds for θ_{MIR} and higher bounds for θ_{VPIN}

We remark in **Tables 15 18** that compared to previous deep search:

Futures	Recall	Precision	Precision+recall	θ_{MIR}	n	ω (buckets)	Classifier	θ_{VPIN}
ES	0.9421	0.9541	1.8962	0.015	30	2500	Student	0.99
EC	0.9080	0.9644	1.8724	0.006	30	2500	Gaussian	0.99
CL	0.9297	0.9806	1.9103	0.016	30	2500	Student	0.99
NQ	0.9076	0.9217	1.8293	0.02	50	2500	Student	0.999
YM	0.9460	0.9696	1.9156	0.015	50	2500	Gaussian	0.99

Table 15.
Best parameters maximizing precision+recall rate for different futures and last bar price structure allowing lower bounds for θ_{MIR} and higher bounds for θ_{VPIN}.

- There are changes only for NQ and YM instruments in, respectively, last, median, and mean bar price structures and first bar price structure, where θ_{VPIN} equals 0.999.
- There is no general trend for precision or recall rates with the increase of θ_{VPIN}.
- On average median bar price structure has the best precision+recall rate.

3.2.7 Benchmark with a "naive" classifier

We remark the following for the "naive" classifier (**Table 19**):

- It has worse results than VPIN on ES and YM cases.
- It has comparable results than VPIN on NQ case.

Futures	Recall	Precision	Precision+recall	θ_{MIR}	n	ω (buckets)	Classifier	θ_{VPIN}
ES	0.9404	0.9402	1.8806	0.015	30	2500	Gaussian	0.99
EC	0.9127	0.9681	1.8808	0.006	30	2500	Student	0.99
CL	0.9232	0.9728	1.8960	0.016	30	2500	Student	0.99
NQ	0.8291	0.9833	1.8124	0.01	30	2500	Student	0.99
YM	0.9341	0.9872	1.9213	0.015	50	2500	Gaussian	0.999

Table 16.
Best parameters maximizing precision+recall rate for different futures and first bar price structure allowing lower bounds for θ_{MIR} and higher bounds for θ_{VPIN}.

Futures	Recall	Precision	Precision+recall	θ_{MIR}	n	ω (buckets)	Classifier	θ_{VPIN}
ES	0.9499	0.9498	1.8997	0.015	30	2500	Student	0.99
EC	0.9037	0.9717	1.8754	0.006	30	2500	Student	0.99
CL	0.9265	0.9718	1.8983	0.016	30	2500	Student	0.99
NQ	0.8881	0.9525	1.8406	0.02	30	2500	Student	0.999
YM	0.9829	0.9427	1.9256	0.015	30	2500	Gaussian	0.99

Table 17.
Best parameters maximizing precision+recall rate for different futures and median bar price structure allowing lower bounds for θ_{MIR} and higher bounds for θ_{VPIN}.

Futures	Recall	Precision	Precision+recall	θ_{MIR}	n	ω (buckets)	Classifier	θ_{VPIN}
ES	0.9526	0.9454	1.8980	0.015	30	2500	Student	0.99
EC	0.9058	0.9691	1.8749	0.006	30	2500	Student	0.99
CL	0.9302	0.9670	1.8972	0.016	30	2500	Gaussian	0.99
NQ	0.9188	0.9150	1.8338	0.02	40	2500	Gaussian	0.999
YM	0.9446	0.9779	1.9225	0.015	60	2500	Gaussian	0.99

Table 18.
Best parameters maximizing precision+recall rate for different futures and mean bar price structure allowing lower bounds for θ_{MIR} and higher bounds for θ_{VPIN}.

Futures	Recall	Precision	Precision+recall	θ_{MIR}	n	ω (buckets)
ES	1	0.7483	1.7483	0.01	40	2500
EC	1	0.9999	1.9999	0.001	60	2500
CL	1	0.9995	1.9995	0.01	40	2500
NQ	1	0.8465	1.8465	0.01	30	2500
YM	1	0.6892	1.6892	0.01	40	2500

Table 19.
Best parameters maximising precision+recall rate for different futures for the naive classifier allowing lower bounds for θ_{MIR}.

- It has better results than VPIN on EC and CL cases, where the flash crash is not really effective.
- It reaches obviously best local results on lowest MIR bound of the deep search.

We may partially conclude that:

- VPIN has an interesting predictive behavior on flash events of magnitude far lower (around 1.5%) than what would be considered as a crash for specific financial instrument (relatively liquid such as NQ, YM, or ES).
- But VPIN has poor results comparable to those of a "naive" classifier (precision +recall rate inferior to 1.2) on flash crash events for these financial instruments.
- For other instruments such as CL or EC, VPIN behaves worse than a naive classifier for these flash events. On flash events of higher amplitude (at least 1.5%), VPIN behaves better than a "naive" classifier for CL instrument.

4. VPIN sensitivity to the starting point of a data set

In this section, first we present the problem of VPIN's sensitivity to the starting point of the bucketing process. Second, we present different calibrations to test its sensitivity. Third we make a summary of our results.

4.1 The problem

VPIN received among critics one which is important to precisely assess. Indeed, Bodarenko and Anderson [7] pointed out in their work that VPIN is sensitive to the starting point of the bucketing process. More precisely, if one removes the first buckets of the data set, results change. It is indeed right. We would like to know to which extent one can or cannot mitigate this effect. One idea is to test the different price bar structures. Indeed a bar structure influences trade imbalance and thus influences the appearance of VPIN events.

4.1.1 Methodology

There are at least two interesting ways of analyzing the sensitivity to the starting point of a data set:

- Study the sensitivity of best precision+recall rate to the number of trades erased and to the bar price option.
- Given one set of local optimal parameters, study the sensitivity of precision and recall rates to bar price option and data removed.

We have removed $l \in 0, 1000, 2000, 3000$ number of bars to study the sensitivity in the two previous cases, which corresponds to several hours of trading data removed. Indeed one does not want to erase first flash crash detected in the data set and erase more buckets than the average prediction length to detect it. Moreover we would like to study to which extent VPIN is locally sensitive.

4.2 Summary of results

4.2.1 Sensitivity of precision+recall rate

We summarize in **Table 20** for each bar price structure the average percentage change of local new best precision+recall rates with the number of bar erased.

We remark the following:

- The sensitivity mentioned by Bodarenko and Anderson does exist.
- Its amplitude is not very big, at least for best precision+recall rate, as the maximum change is about 6%.
- Median bar price structure is far less sensitive than other price structure.

Bar price structure	1000 bars erased	2000 bars erased	3000 bars erased
Last	3.089	2.166	0.939
First	2.410	3.649	6.727
Median	0.611	0.801	0.781
Mean	1.348	2.149	3.944

Table 20.
Average absolute percentage change of local best precision+recall rates with the number of bar erased for each bar price structure.

Bar price structure	1000 bars erased	2000 bars erased	3000 bars erased
Last	1.192	1.171	1.067
First	1.612	1.725	1.049
Median	3.514	3.137	1.396
Mean	2.648	3.180	2.489

Table 21.
Average absolute percentage change of local best precision+recall rates with the number of bar erased for each bar price structure.

4.2.2 Sensitivity to local best parameter choice

In **Table 21** we summarize for each bar price structure the average percentabe change of the initial local best precision+recall rates with the number of bar erased.

We remark the following:

- Again the amplitude of the sensitivity is not very large as the maximum change is about 3.5%.

- Last bar price structure is less sensitive than other price structure to this phenomenon.

5. Conclusion

In this last section, we present first a general summary of our findings. Then we propose new suggestion of research concerning this precise subject.

5.1 Summary of results

We found that:

- VPIN has interesting predictive power (i.e., better than a naive algorithm and at least of local prediction+recall maximum higher than 1.2) for flash events of lower amplitude than flash crashes (about 1.5%) for a certain class of instruments, where flash crashes are at least present (which is not the case for currency Euro FX or Energy Light Crude NYMEX).

- VPIN is sensitive to the starting point of computation, but the amplitude of this sensitivity is not really high. For practice, which means not changing local best parameters while erasing some data, last bar price structure is the least sensitive to this phenomenon.

5.2 Suggestion for further studies

For further studies, this might be worth analyzing:

- Define a bigger constraint to capture crashes taking into account, for example, their V-shape. It would indeed filter out more events and enable analyzing more accurately which kind of crash VPIN predicts better.

- Benchmark within this framework other predictive tools between them (VIX with a naive algorithm, with VPIN, etc.).

- Analyze VPIN time-clock version predictive power.

- If previous predictive power of lower amplitude flash events is interesting for practitioners, analyze more precisely parameters that would be interesting for them.

- Describe more precisely to which class of financial instrument VPIN predictive power is most effective (if such one is worth being more studied for practitioners).

- Define a normalization of events defining crash events within a whole cluster of instruments. It is not easy to put in place as instruments are more or less correlated by crashes and response times are not trivial to analyze, but it would be also interesting indeed to assess prediction quality on common events shared by different instruments of a same cluster. It would make it possible to see whether or not VPIN predictive power is effective beyond different financial instruments embedding different aspects of the financial world to which VPIN is sensitive to.

- This area of research studies a very particular class of events: those that are potentially very rare. Taking into account this setting and that the algorithms used are fed with previous information and are sensitive to the starting point of computation, is it possible to build a consistent cross-validation approach? This aspect has not been treated yet as others needed to be first addressed, but it is still important to be studied.

Appendix

See **Table 22**.

Symbol	Description	Exchange	Class	Volume
ES	S&P500 E-mini	CME	Equity	478,029
EC	Euro FX	CME	Currency	188,837
CL	Light Crude NYMEX	NYMEX	Energy	165,208
YM	Dow Jones E-mini	CBOT	Equity	110,122
NQ	Nasdaq 100	CME	Equity	173,211

Table 22.
List of future contracts and their total volume of trades from January 2007 to July 2012.

Author details

Antoine Bambade[1*] and Kesheng Wu[2]

1 École Polytechnique (Palaiseau), France

2 Lawrence Berkeley National Laboratory, Scientific Data Management (SDM) group, USA

*Address all correspondence to: antoine.bambade@polytechnique.edu

References

[1] Easley D, de Prado ML, O'Hara M. Flow toxicity and liquidity in a high frequency world. Review of Financial Studies. 2012;**25**(5):1457-1493

[2] Easley D, de Prado ML, O'Hara M. The microstructure of the 'flash crash': Flow toxicity, liquidity, crashes and the probability of informed trading. The Journal of Portfolio Management. 2011; **37**(2):118-128

[3] Zheng Y. VPIN and the China's circuit-breaker. International Journal of Economics and Finance. 2017;**9**(12)

[4] Abad D, Yagüe J. From PIN to VPIN: An introduction to order flow toxicity. The Spanish Review of Financial Economics. 2011;**6**(2):8-13. Johnson School Research Paper Series No. 10-2011

[5] Wu K, Bethel EW, Gu M, Leinweber D, Rübel O. A big data approach to analyzing market volatility. Algorithmic Finance. 2013;**2**(3–4):241-267

[6] Easley D, de Prado ML, O'Hara M. The exchange of flow toxicity. The Journal of Trading. 2011;**6**(2):8-13. Johnson School Research Paper Series No. 10-2011

[7] Andersen TG, Bondarenko O. VPIN and the flash crash. The Journal of Financial Markets. 2014;**17**:1-46

[8] Andersen TG, Bondarenko O. Reflecting on the VPIN dispute. Journal of Financial Markets. 2014;**17**:53-64

[9] Andersen TG, Bondarenko O. Assessing measures of order flow toxicity and early warning signals for market turbulence. Review of Finance. 2015;**19**:1-54

[10] Abad D, Massot M, Pascual R. Evaluating VPIN as a trigger for single-stock circuit breakers. Journal of Banking and Finance. 2017;**86**(C):21-36

[11] Pöppe T, Moss S, Schiereck D. The sensitivity of VPIN to the choice of trade classification algorithm. Journal of Banking and Finance. 2016;**73**:165-181

[12] Easley D, Engle RF, O'Hara M, Wu L. Time-varying arrival rates of informed and uninformed trades. Journal of Financial Econometrics. 2008;**6**(2):171-207

[13] Easley D, Kiefer NM, O'Hara M, Paperman JB. Liquidity, information, and infrequently traded stocks. Journal of Finance. 1996;**51**(4):1405-1436

[14] Easley D, de Prado ML, O'Hara M. The volume clock: Insights into the high frequency paradigm. Journal of Portfolio Management. Vol. 39, No. 1, (01 Sep Fall). 11

[15] Ke W-C, Lin H-WW. An Improved Version of the Volume-Synchronized Probability of Informed Trading (VPIN)

[16] Easley D, de Prado ML, O'Hara M. An Improved Version of the Volume-Synchronized Probability of Informed Trading (VPIN): A Comment

Chapter 6

Artificial Intelligence Data Science Methodology for Earth Observation

Corneliu Octavian Dumitru, Gottfried Schwarz, Fabien Castel, Jose Lorenzo and Mihai Datcu

Abstract

This chapter describes a Copernicus Access Platform Intermediate Layers Small-Scale Demonstrator, which is a general platform for the handling, analysis, and interpretation of Earth observation satellite images, mainly exploiting big data of the European Copernicus Programme by artificial intelligence (AI) methods. From 2020, the platform will be applied at a regional and national level to various use cases such as urban expansion, forest health, and natural disasters. Its workflows allow the selection of satellite images from data archives, the extraction of useful information from the metadata, the generation of descriptors for each individual image, the ingestion of image and descriptor data into a common database, the assignment of semantic content labels to image patches, and the possibility to search and to retrieve similar content-related image patches. The main two components, namely, data mining and data fusion, are detailed and validated. The most important contributions of this chapter are the integration of these two components with a Copernicus platform on top of the European DIAS system, for the purpose of large-scale Earth observation image annotation, and the measurement of the clustering and classification performances of various Copernicus Sentinel and third-party mission data. The average classification accuracy is ranging from 80 to 95% depending on the type of images.

Keywords: Earth observation, machine learning, data mining, Copernicus Programme, TerraSAR-X

1. Introduction

Typical shortcomings of current image analysis tools are the lack of content understanding. This becomes apparent with current developments in Earth observation and data analysis [1]. In this chapter, we therefore concentrate on artificial intelligence (AI) applications and our solution strategies as our main objectives in the field of remote sensing, i.e., the acquisition and semantic interpretation of instrument data from remote platforms such as aircraft or satellites observing, for instance, atmospheric phenomena on Earth for weather prediction—or icebergs drifting in arctic waters endangering maritime transport. In particular, we will describe the exploitation of imaging data acquired by Earth-observing satellites and their sensors.

These satellites may either circle about the Earth (mostly on low polar Earth orbits) or be operated from stationary or slowly moving points high above our planet (on so-called geostationary or geosynchronous orbits). Typical examples are Earth-observing and meteorological satellites. All these instruments have been designed with dedicated goals that, as a rule, can only be fulfilled by systematic and interactive data processing and data interpretation on the ground. The processing and data analysis chains are then the main candidates where one can and shall apply modern data science approaches (e.g., machine learning and artificial intelligence) in order to fully exploit the full information content of the sensor data.

In general, we have quite a number of different sensors installed on satellites. These include passive instruments observing the backscattered solar illumination or thermal emissions from the Earth—or active imaging instruments (transmitting and receiving light pulses or radio signals toward and from the target area being observed). For the ease of understanding, we will limit ourselves to optical sensors operating in the visible and infrared spectral ranges and to radar sensors applying synthetic-aperture radar (SAR) concepts [2, 3]. These instruments provide large-scale images with a typical spatial resolution of 1–40 m per pixel. The images can be acquired from spacecraft orbits that cover the Earth completely with well-defined repeat cycles.

After being transmitted to the ground, the image data will have to undergo systematic processing steps. Typically, the processing schemes follow a stepwise approach where for all steps the image data are accompanied by the necessary descriptor data (metadata). The processing chains start with what we call level-0 data consisting of reordered and annotated detector data; level-1 data provide calibrated sensor data, while level-2 data contain data in commonly known physical units preferably on regular spatial or map grids. Then level-3 data are higher-level products such as thematic maps or time series results (obtained by merging or concatenation of several individual images) or similar operations. Finally, users can apply additional interactive processing steps on their own or exploit available software/platform concepts [4].

This principle of ordered value-adding requires well-established techniques for data management, batch processing and databases, local and distributed (cloud) processing, understanding of the information flow, experience with learning principles, knowledge extraction from image and library data, and discovery of image semantics. At present, typical data sources with easy access are publicly available scientific image data provided by the European Copernicus mission with its Sentinel satellites [5, 6] as well as high-resolution remote sensing images [7, 8]. The European Sentinel satellites comprise among others a constellation of SAR imagers (i.e., Sentinel-1A/Sentinel-1B providing typically large radar images, with a ground sampling distance of 20 meters and selectable horizontal and vertical polarizations), and a constellation of optical imagers (i.e., Sentinel-2A/Sentinel-2B delivering typically large multispectral images with 13 different bands and a ground resolution—depending on the bands—of 10–60 m). This space segment of the Copernicus mission is complemented by systematic level-1 and level-2 image data processing on the ground and by support environments that serve as comfortable platforms for further data handling and interpretation covering all aspects of applied data science. These approaches then pave the way for deeper semantic data analysis and understanding as typically required in Earth observation for crop yield predictions, atmospheric research, etc.

The design of Earth observation (EO) missions as constellations of several satellites brings important advantages. However, this is not the case for some of the most popular EO missions. **Figure 1** shows typical TerraSAR-X and Copernicus Sentinel overpasses from different orbits and their target areas.

TerraSAR-X flies on a polar Sun-synchronous circular dawn-dusk orbit. This satellite shares its orbit plane with its twin satellite TanDEM-X (keeping a 97.44°

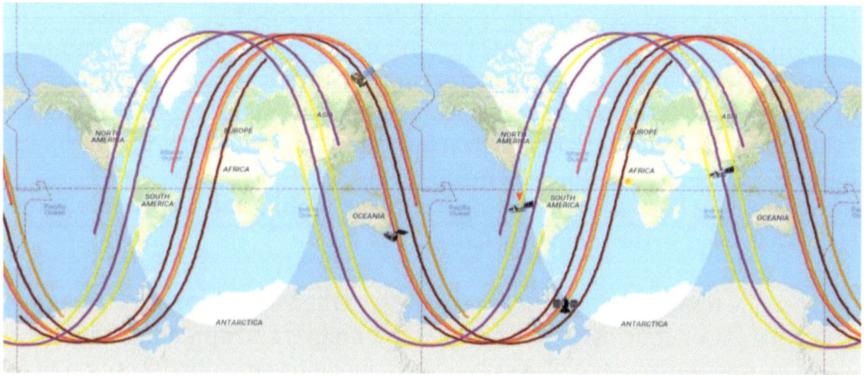

Figure 1.
Satellite overpasses of Sentinel-1A/Sentinel-1B, Sentinel-2A/Sentinel-2B, and TerraSAR-X (on 23th of August 2018 starting at 14:02 UT) [12].

orbital phasing difference) and a repeat cycle of 11 days with 167 orbits per cycle. Due to its flexibility, TerraSAR-X can cover any point on Earth within a maximum of 4.5 days and 90% of the Earth's surface within 2 days [9].

The Sentinel-1 satellites fly on a near-polar, Sun-synchronous orbit, too. The satellite constellations (comprising Sentinel-1A and Sentinel-1B) share the same orbit plane with a 180° orbital phasing difference and a repeat cycle of 6 days with 175 orbits per cycle. Sentinel-1 can cover the equator on 3 days, the Artic on less than 1 day, and Europe, Canada, and shipping routes in 1–3 days [10].

Like the Sentinel-1 constellation, the Sentinel-2 constellations (comprising Sentinel-2A and Sentinel-2B) share the same orbit with a separation of 180°. The repeat cycle is 5 days with 143 orbits per cycle. Sentinel-2 can cover the equator on 5 days under cloud-free conditions and in 2–3 days at mid-latitudes [11].

When selecting data for fusion, we have to constrain ourselves to data acquired as close as possible in time.

These data handling approaches are typical for recent advances in big data scenarios in distributed systems on the web (e.g., with high data volumes and throughput rates, conventional and innovative data processing steps, additional necessary tools and environments, and greater user expectations). In our case, this affects the tasks of image processing (e.g., data fusion), image understanding, and comparisons with physical models. This can also be seen when we look at the evolution of satellite data analysis. While early concepts started with data being transferred to algorithms, current systems often transfer data to archives, and future systems may support more and more distributed systems.

A typical example is the full functionality offered by machine learning tools, while the basic ideas of future data science aspects for Earth observation as seen by the European Space Agency can be found in [13]. In our case, we are interested in applying more theoretical data science, machine learning, and artificial intelligence (for instance, deep learning, powerful classification maps, and prediction results) together with interactive visualization on various information levels. These ideas will be dealt with below for three remote sensing scenarios as detailed in [14]:

- Urban monitoring (urban growth and sprawl, urban classification, and semantic indicators)
- Quantitative interpretation of forested areas
- Disaster monitoring (earthquakes, inundations, mud slides, etc.)

Here traceable products yielding quantitative data about physical phenomena, change maps, and change predictions are among our primary goals. Of course, we have to consider the implementation effort as well as the attainable accuracy of our products. For each scenario dealt with below, the reader should try to understand what the additional value of machine learning, artificial intelligence, and comprehensive use of data science concepts brings about.

The basic terms of machine learning, artificial intelligence, and data science shall be understood in the following sense:

- We use the term "machine learning" mainly when we talk about learning target category parameters derived from selected images and applying these parameters to other examples. Currently, we see much progress by "deep" techniques (e.g., deep learning [15, 16]). An important point is the selection of reliable reference data for traceable validation and verification of the methods.

- "Artificial intelligence" describes how machine learning results are exploited for further use. Typically this includes recognizing and being aware of typical situations, making decisions based on the recognized high-level parameters, and predicting future developments. To this end, one can profit from external databases complementing machine learning results.

- "Data science" covers the entire field of comprehensive data management and tools, machine learning, and artificial intelligence. This includes topics like distributed processing, monitoring of workflows, visualization techniques, and performance monitoring. Even seemingly trivial tasks (e.g., accessing and handling of data) may belong to data science. However, remote sensing still is in urgent need of efficient tools to familiarize the user community with remote sensing opportunities.

When we look at remote sensing in more detail, we currently see many efforts to transform sensor data to physical quantities that can be exploited for quantitative analysis or modeling. If we accomplish this, we can combine measured data with physical models and find quantitative parameters for predictions.

In the following, we describe how we applied these concepts in a research project funded by the European Union [17]; the project's main objective is to allow the creation of added value from Copernicus data through the provisioning of modeling and analytics tools for data collection, processing, storage, and access that are provided by the Copernicus Data and Information Access Services (DIAS) [18] and creating a data science workflow where sub-images (image chips) are annotated, administered, and validated based on their assigned semantic labels [19].

The chapter is organized in seven main sections. Section 2 explains the CANDELA platform used for prototyping EO applications, while Section 3 describes the characteristics of the data set. Section 4 presents typical examples which a user can obtain when using the platform from Section 2 and the data set from Section 3. Section 5 illustrates the perspectives in EO data science workflows and Section 6 summarizes our conclusions, while Section 7 contains the future work. The chapter ends with acknowledgments and a list of references.

2. The CANDELA platform

CANDELA's main objective is the creation of additional value from Copernicus data through the provisioning of modeling and analytics tools provided that the

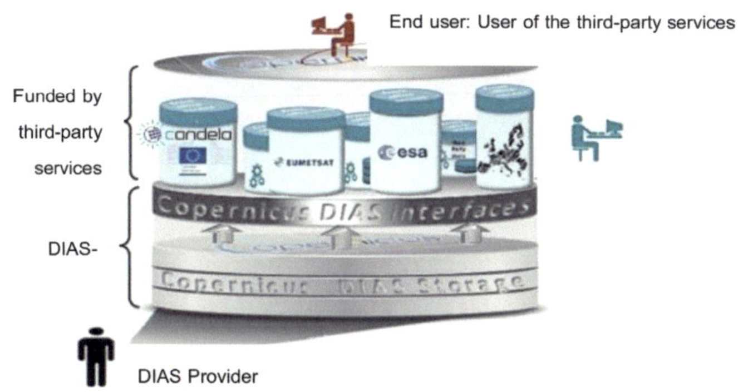

Figure 2.
CANDELA platform [17].

tasks of data collection, processing, storage, and access will be carried out by the Copernicus Data Information and Access Service [18]. The corresponding flowchart is presented in **Figure 2** and in [17]. In the end, after the integration of all components, CANDELA will be deployed on top of DIAS.

The CANDELA platform [17] allows prototyping of EO applications by applying efficient data retrieval, data mining augmented with machine learning techniques, as well as interoperability in order to fully benefit from the available assets and to add more value to the satellite data. It also helps to interactively detect objects or structures and to classify land cover categories.

The implementation of the platform is putting in place a set of powerful tools in artificial intelligence environments (e.g., with machine learning and deep learning). These tools have as their objectives:

- To process large volumes of EO data and to perform data analytics
- To extract the information content from the EO data based on data mining
- To fuse various EO sensors in order to increase and to complement the information extracted from different sensors
- To apply deep learning to detect changes in EO data
- To semantically search and index our EO image catalog

From this list of objectives, we focus on two of them, namely, data mining and data fusion (see **Figure 3**). Our goal is to simplify data access and to analyze large volumes of EO data without specific knowledge about the processing of EO data and to fuse the outputs for content exploration.

For the development of the data mining component, we started from [20], and we improved the cascaded active learning system of [21] for typical Copernicus Earth observation images. Its implementation, test, and validation aim at automated knowledge extraction and image content interpretation. The results are presented in Section 4.1.

Regarding data fusion, a new sub-component had to be developed within data mining. This new sub-component fuses multispectral and SAR images. There are two types of fusions; one is performed at the feature level and the other one at the semantic level. The results are shown in Section 4.2 for feature-level fusion.

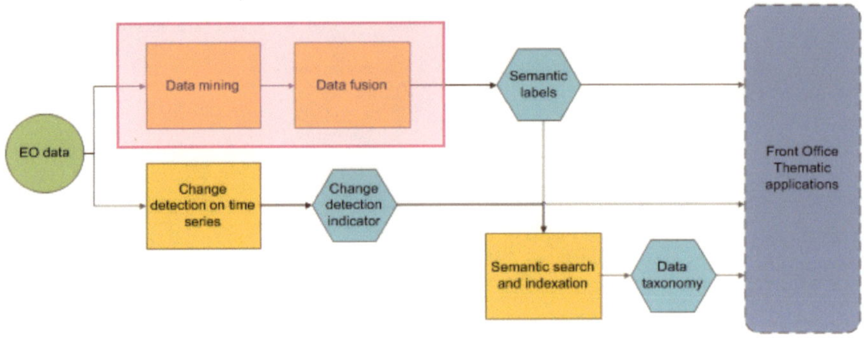

Figure 3.
Block diagram of the CANDELA platform modules [17].

3. Data set description for CANDELA

Our main data sets extracted from different instruments are Earth's surface images of the European Copernicus Programme (e.g., Sentinel-1 and Sentinel-2). Sentinel-1 is a twin satellite synthetic-aperture radar configuration, while Sentinel-2 is also a twin satellite configuration, each carrying a multispectral imager [22, 23].

There are three reasons why we are selecting and using Sentinel-1 and Sentinel-2 images. Firstly, we can recognize different target area details in overlapping radar and optical images complementing each other with rapid succession. Secondly, individually selectable Sentinel-1 and Sentinel-2 images can be rectified and co-aligned by publicly available toolbox routines offered by ESA allowing a straightforward image comparison or image fusion. Thirdly, all Sentinel instruments are totally openly available to the EO community. Many publications (dedicated conferences [1, 24–26]) already describe newly discovered Earth's surface characteristics derived from the individual instruments.

Furthermore, the long-term operations of the Sentinel satellites allow the interpretation of image time series or even the combination of time series data with external supplementary data via additional data mining and data fusion tools [1, 25, 26].

Besides these data sets, we include other third-party EO mission data sets as specified by CANDELA users (e.g., TerraSAR-X and WorldView).

3.1 Sentinel-1 data

The Sentinel-1 mission comprises a constellation of two satellites (launched on April 1, 2014, and on April 25, 2016), operating in C-band for synthetic-aperture radar imaging. SAR has the advantage of operating at wavelengths not impeded by thin cloud cover, or a lack of solar illumination, and can acquire data over a selected area during day- or nighttime under nearly no weather condition restrictions. The repeat period of each satellite is 12 days; that means every 6 days there is an acquisition by one of the two satellites.

The Sentinel-1 characteristics are presented in detail in [22]. From the multitude of parameters/configurations that exist for Sentinel-1, we have selected as examples the following configurations based on data availability, the CANDELA use cases, and our previous experiments: level-1 Ground Range Detected (GRD) products with high resolution (HR) taken routinely in Interferometric Wide (IW) swath mode. These products/data are produced (prior to geo-coding) with a pixel spacing of 10×10 m and correspond to about five looks and a resolution (range × azimuth) of

20 × 22 m. They have a nearly uniform signal-to-noise ratio (SNR) and also a stable distributed target ambiguity ratio (DTAR). For these products, the data are provided in dual polarization, VV and VH for land and HH and HV for polar target areas.

3.2 Sentinel-2 data

The Sentinel-2 mission (like Sentinel-1) comprises a constellation of two satellites (launched on June 23, 2015, and on March 7, 2017) able to collect multispectral data and is affected by the weather conditions (e.g., cloud cover). The repeat period of each satellite is 10 days; that means every 5 days there is an acquisition of one of the two satellites, thus providing a high revisit frequency.

Each Sentinel-2 satellite carries a multispectral instrument with 13 spectral channels (in the visible/near-infrared and shortwave infrared spectral range) and with 290 km swath width. The Sentinel-2 characteristics are presented in detail in [23]. This also applies to level-1 data; level-1C of these products are radiometrically and geometrically corrected images with orthorectification and spatial registration on a global reference system with sub-pixel accuracy. Since the product size is very large, each image is divided into several quadrants in UTM WGS84 projection. The average size of a quadrant is 10,980 × 10,980 pixels (rows × columns). For visualization, the RGB bands (B04, B03, and B02) were used to generate a quick-look quadrant image. For feature extraction, the user can choose different band combinations.

3.3 Third-party mission data

From the available third-party mission data sets, we selected for demonstration four pairs of multi-sensor images of TerraSAR-X and WorldView-2 [27].

TerraSAR-X is a German radar satellite launched in June 2007, followed by its TanDEM-X twin in 2010. Both operate in X-band and are side-looking SAR instruments that offer a wide selection of operating modes and product generation options [7]. TerraSAR-X has a revisit cycle of 11 days on the Earth's equator. We selected high-resolution spotlight mode images because they provide the highest-resolution data of the target areas. As for the product generation options, we took enhanced ellipsoid corrected (EEC) and radiometrically enhanced (RE) data. Finally, we took horizontally polarized (HH) or vertically polarized (VV) images, as this option is most frequently used. The images have a pixel spacing of 1.25 m and a resolution of 2.9 m with WGS-84 map projection. The average size of the images is 8000 rows × 9600 columns.

In contrast, WorldView-2 provides a single panchromatic band and eight multispectral bands. It was launched in October 2009 to become a DigitalGlobe satellite. The revisit period of the satellite is about 3 days on the Earth's equator [28]. The resolution for the panchromatic band is 0.46 m and for multispectral bands is 1.87 m. The map projection of WorldView-2 is, again, WGS-84, and the size of these images (on average) for panchromatic images is 47,000 × 37,000 pixels (rows × columns) and for multispectral images is 11,000 × 9000 pixels (rows × columns).

4. Typical CANDELA examples

4.1 Data mining by machine learning

In EO data mining, a number of researchers have already developed technologies for semantic image understanding [29, 30]. The available web engines are focused on the everyday needs of a broad category of users [31]. A very popular satellite image data mining system is Tomnod from DigitalGlobe or Google Earth, which is targeting general user topics. Especially for EO, there are systems such as LandEX [32] which is a land cover management system, while GeoIRIS [33] is a system that allows the user to refine a given query by iteratively specifying a set of relevant and a set of nonrelevant images. A similar system is IKONA [34] which is using relevance feedback in order to analyze the content of very high-resolution EO images. Further, the knowledge-driven information mining (KIM) system [41] is an example of an active learning system providing semantic interpretation of image content. The KIM concept evolved into the TELEIOS prototype [36], complementing the scope of searching EO images with additional geo-information and in situ data. Finally, a cascaded active learning prototype [21] has been integrated into an operational EO system [20] to interpret the archives of TerraSAR-X images [37].

CANDELA is improving this cascaded active learning system by searching for dedicated algorithms for typical Earth observation images. Its implementation, test, and validation aim at automated knowledge extraction and image content interpretation. The targeted performance characteristics are verified for several typical use cases and tell us more about the potential of dedicated algorithms with respect to general machine learning.

Figures 4–9 depict typical classification maps for TerraSAR-X and Sentinel-1 images together with their respective accuracy (e.g., precision/recall) for the cities of Venice, Italy, and Munich, Germany. Another example is the Dutch part of the Wadden Sea in the Netherlands. The results of the classification map and their accuracy are given in **Figures 10** and **11**.

4.2 Data fusion by machine learning

Currently, what exists in the field of data fusion is a collection of routines/algorithms that can be linked and embedded for various applications. A very well-known

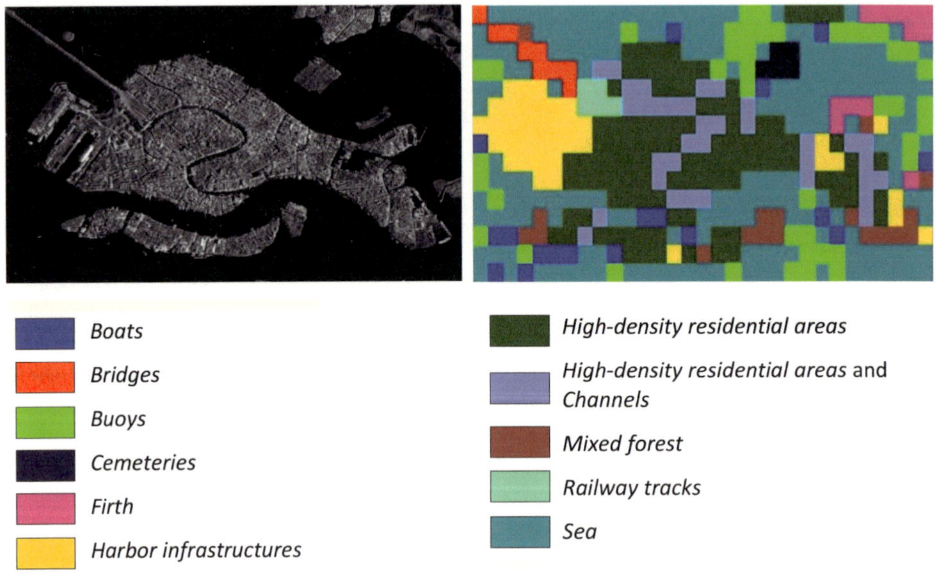

Figure 4.
TerraSAR-X image of Venice, Italy: (left) a quick-look view of the image and (right) the corresponding classification map generated by CANDELA.

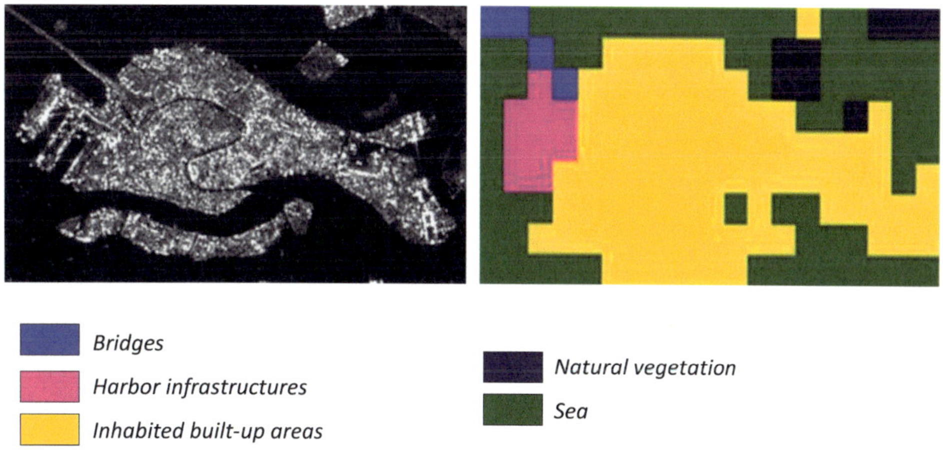

Figure 5.
Sentinel-1 image of Venice, Italy (after selecting the area that is covered by TerraSAR-X from the full Sentinel-1 image): (bottom-left) a quick-look view of the image and (bottom-right) the classification map generated by CANDELA.

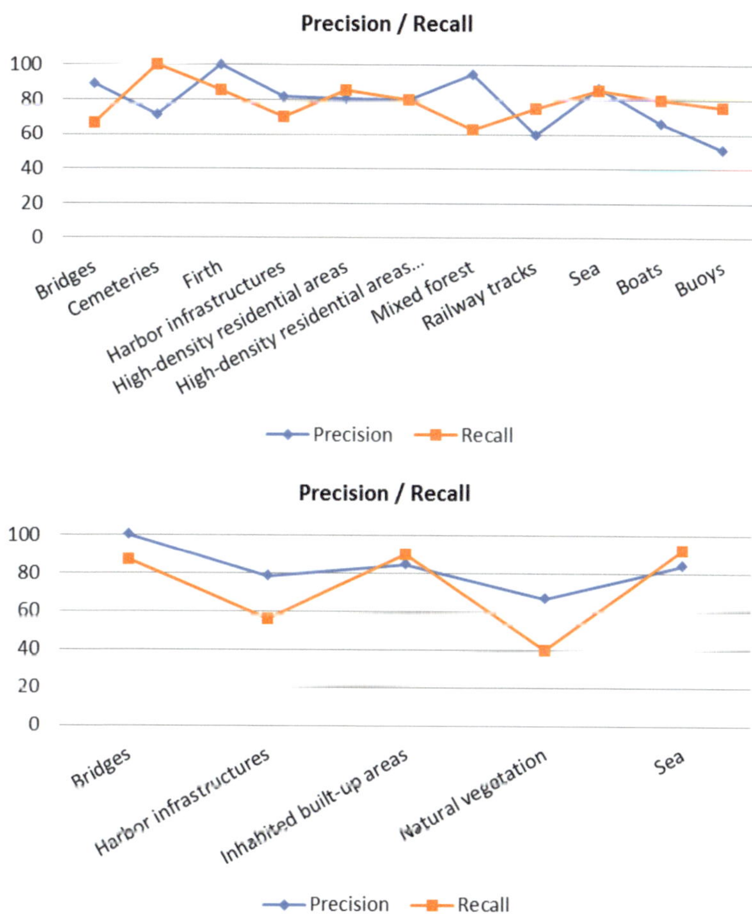

Figure 6.
Classification accuracy (precision/recall) by comparison between TerraSAR-X (top-left) and Sentinel-1 (bottom-right) for the Venice image.

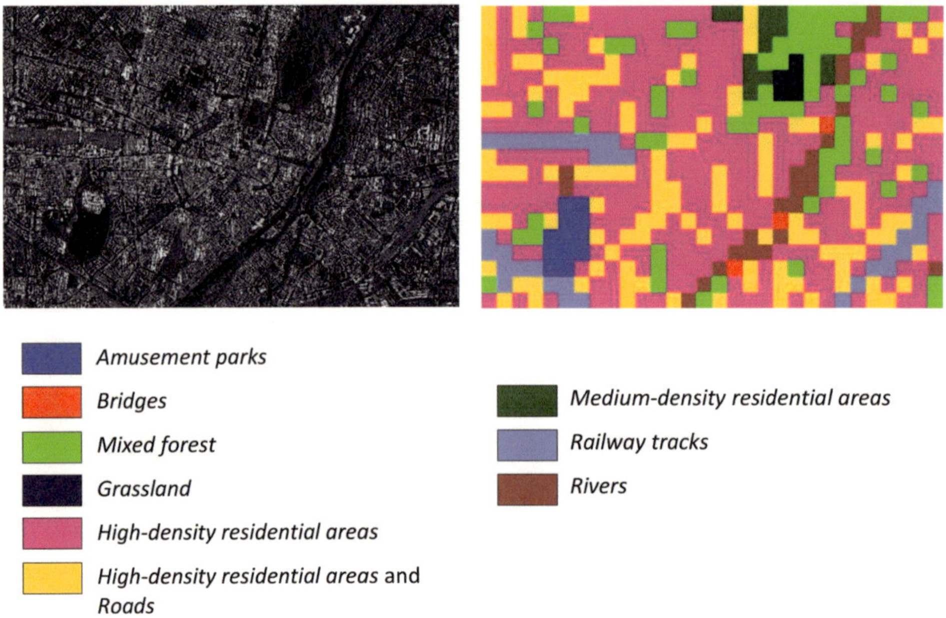

Figure 7.
TerraSAR-X image of Munich, Germany: (left) a quick-look view of the image and (right) the classification map generated by CANDELA.

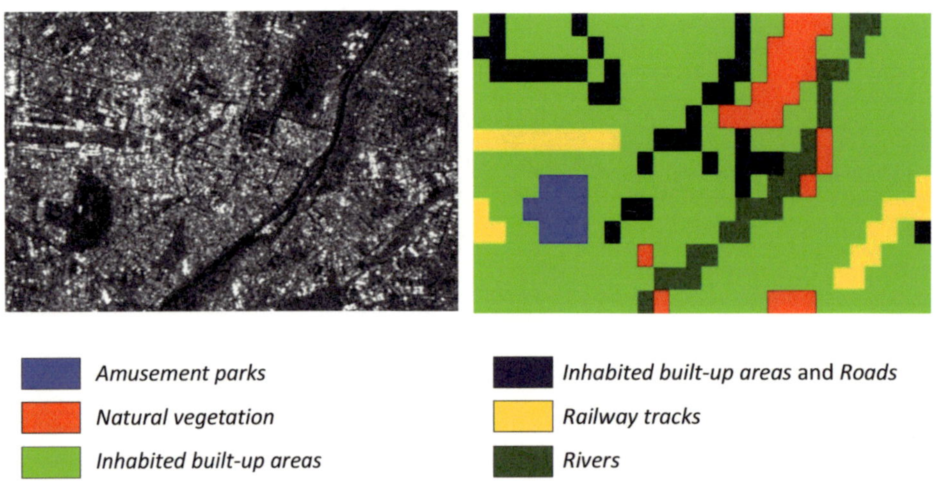

Figure 8.
Sentinel-1 image of Munich, Germany (after selecting the area that is also covered by TerraSAR-X): (bottom-left) a quick-look view of the image and (bottom-right) the classification map generated by CANDELA.

open-source toolbox is Orfeo [38] which provides a large number of state-of-the-art algorithms to process SAR and multispectral images for different applications. Another one is Google Earth [31] that includes a large image database and an expandable number of algorithms that can be used for image processing.

In our case, we need to recognize different target area details in overlapping SAR and multispectral images. For doing this, we selected a number of cities from all over the world. The cities are Bucharest in Romania, Munich in Germany, Venice in Italy, and Washington in the USA. The selection criteria of these cities were the simultaneous availability of these cities covered by the two satellites and the variety of categories that can be found. A difficulty arises when trying to co-align these images, for

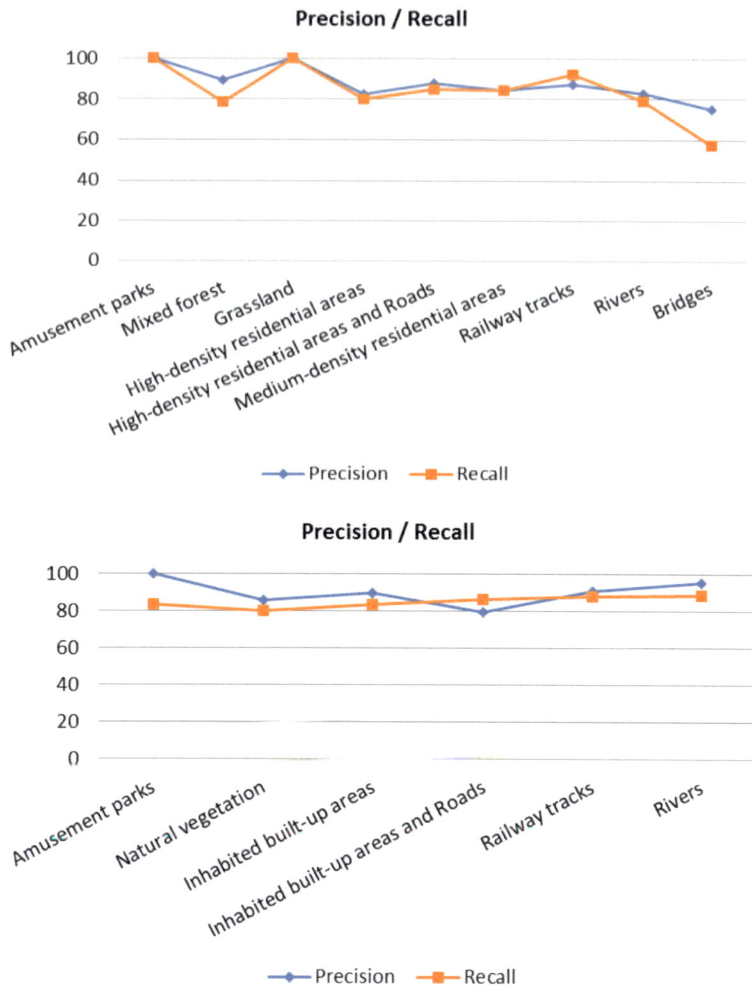

Figure 9.
Classification accuracy (precision/recall) by comparison between TerraSAR-X (top-right) and Sentinel-1 (bottom-left) for the Munich image.

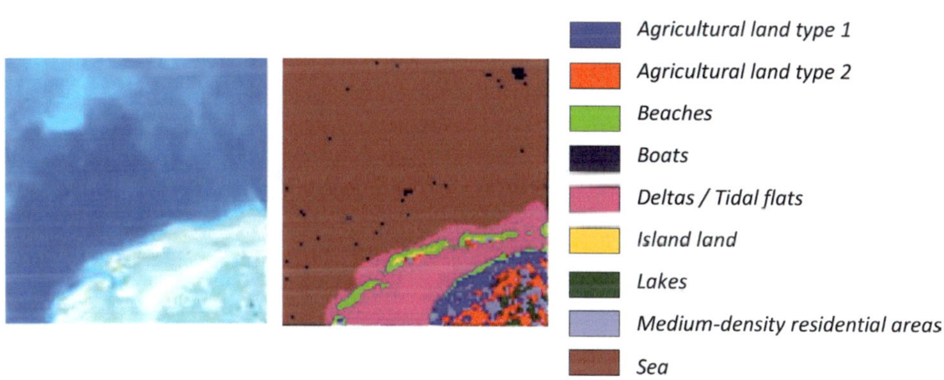

Figure 10.
Sentinel-2 quadrant image of an area of the Dutch Wadden Sea: (left) a quick-look view of the image and (right) the classification map generated by CANDELA.

example, images provided by TerraSAR-X and WorldView-2, because the original data have different pixel spacing. To solve this problem, we resampled the panchromatic WorldView-2 image in order to co-align it with the TerraSAR-X image [27].

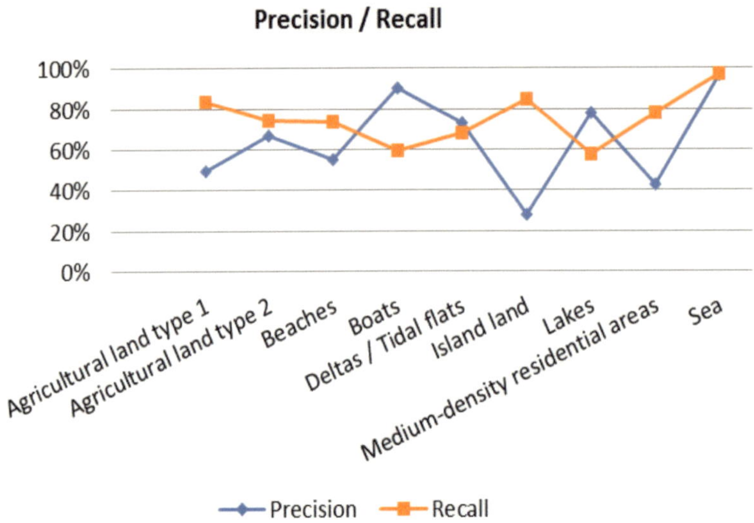

Figure 11.
Classification accuracy (precision/recall) for the Sentinel-2 quadrant image covering an area of the Wadden Sea.

In the case of Sentinel-1 and Sentinel-2, the images can be rectified and co-aligned by publicly available toolbox routines [39]; this allowed us a straightforward image comparison.

While we are accustomed to image fusion as a radiometric combination of multispectral images, a comparably mature level of semantic fusion of SAR images has not been reached yet. In order to remedy the situation, we propose a semantic fusion concept for SAR images, where we combine the semantic image content of two data sets with different characteristics. By exploiting the specific imaging details and the retrievable semantic categories of the two image types, we obtained

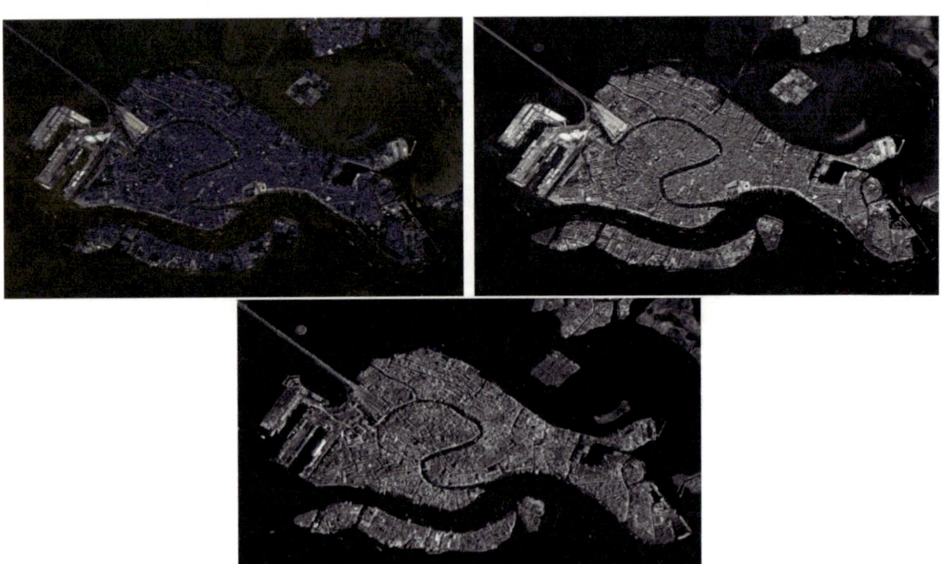

Figure 12.
A multi-sensor data set: multispectral image (top-left side), panchromatic image (top-right side), and TerraSAR-X image (bottom-center) for the city of Venice, Italy.

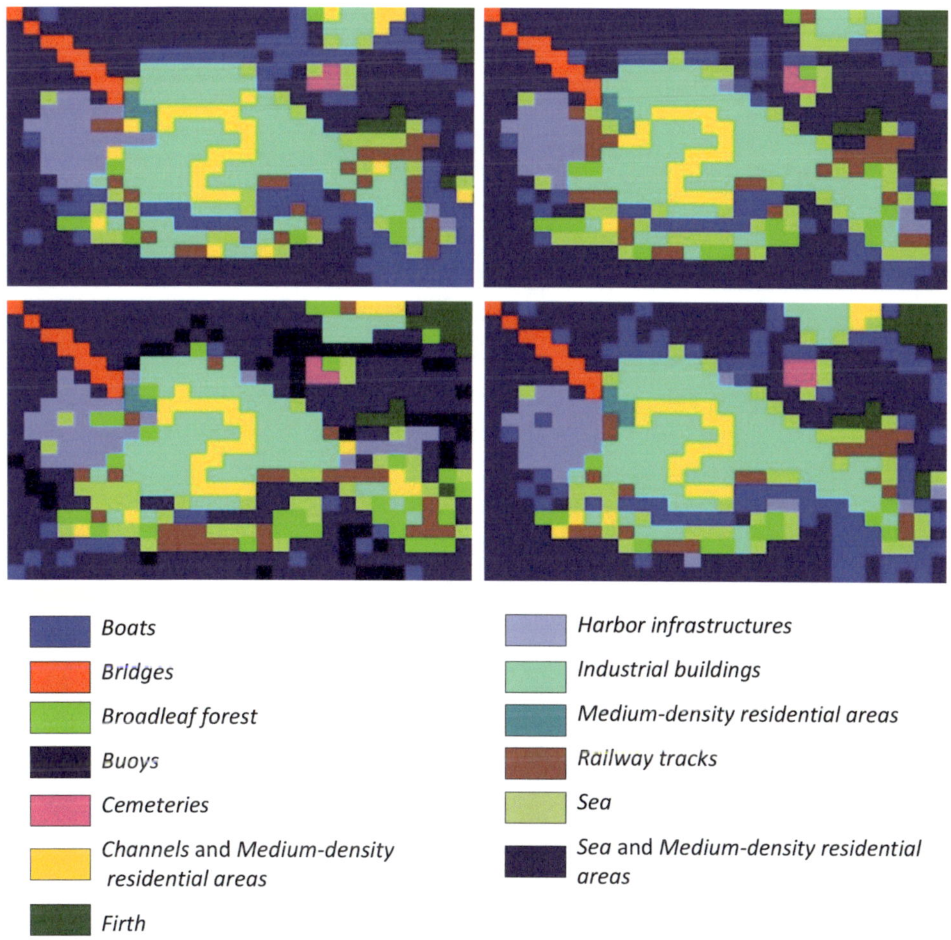

Figure 13.
Classification maps generated using the CANDELA platform for the city of Venice: multispectral image (top-left side), panchromatic image (top-right side), TerraSAR-X image (bottom-left side), and fusion of all three images (bottom-right side).

semantically fused image classification maps that allow us to differentiate between different categories.

Figures 12–14 present the classification maps for each sensor and the fused ones together with their accuracy (e.g., precision/recall) for the city of Venice, while **Figures 15–17** apply to the city of Munich.

For a quantitative assessment, we compared the semantic annotation results with the given reference data set and computed precision/recall for each category and sensor. Analyzing the figures separately, we observed that the average of precision/recall obtained for fused sensor images is higher than the precision/recall of individual sensor images. Unfortunately, there are also cases in which for corresponding image patches tiled from different sensor images, the WorldView-2 annotations have a different semantic classification when compared to the TerraSAR-X results or when a category is missing for one sensor. In our case, in the Venice image, the category “buoys” is only detected in the TerraSAR-X image, and not in the WorldView-2 image. This has a noticeable impact on the performance of the category “boats.” Another example is the category “clouds” that appears in the case of the Munich image that is detected in the WorldView-2 image, but not in the TerraSAR-X image.

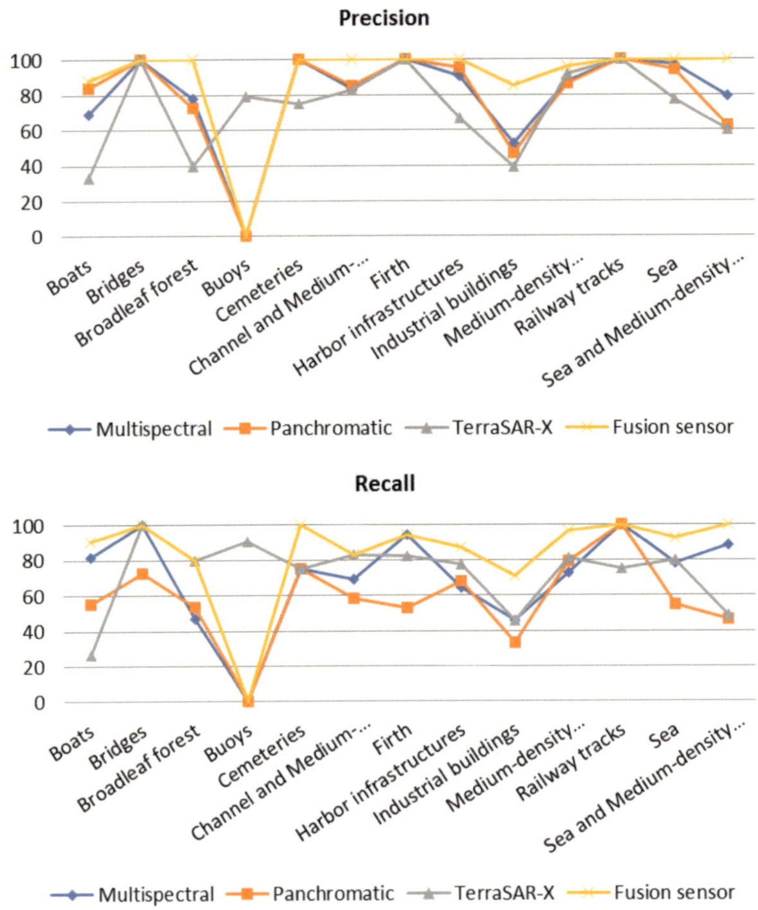

Figure 14.
Classification accuracy (precision/recall) for a selected image taken over the area of Venice using multispectral, panchromatic, and SAR images and also the fused image.

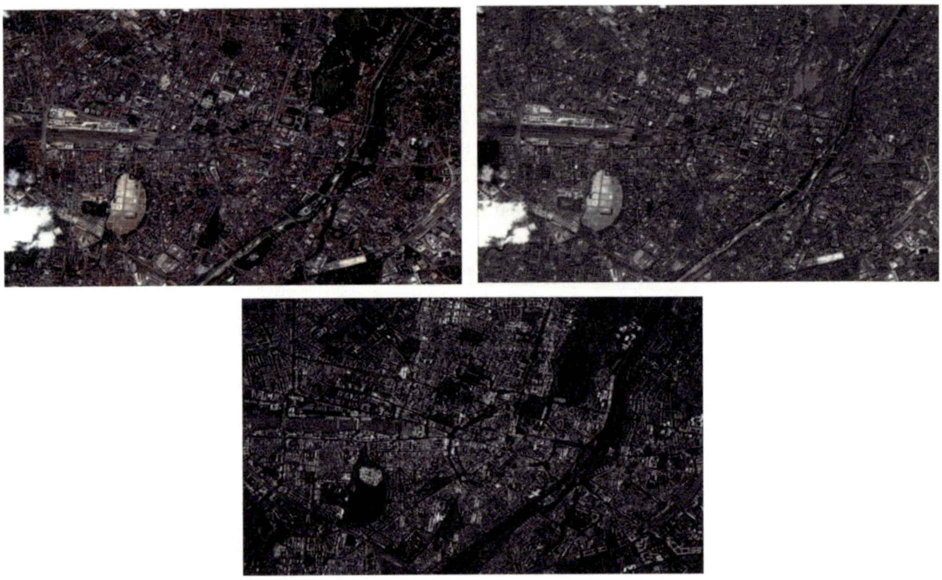

Figure 15.
A multi-sensor data set: multispectral image (top-left side), panchromatic image (top-right side), and TerraSAR-X image (bottom-center) for the city of Munich, Germany.

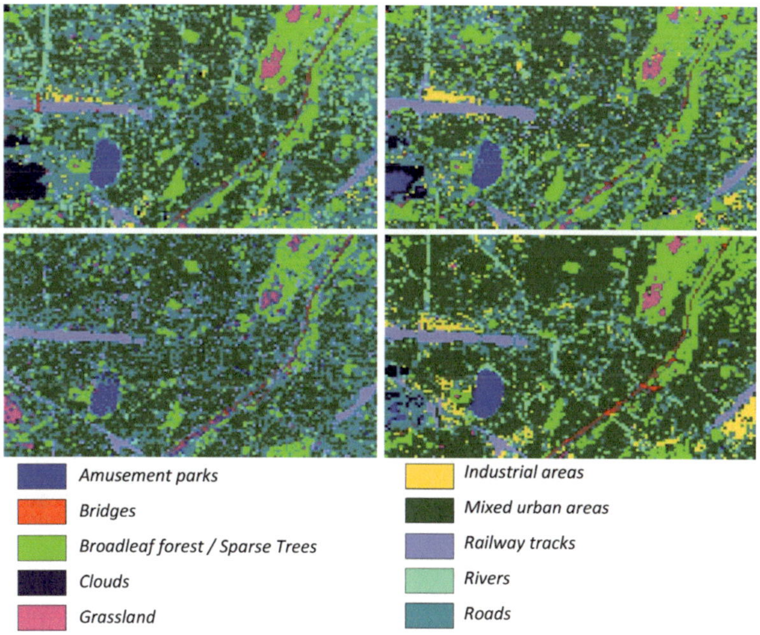

Figure 16.
Classification maps generated using the CANDELA platform for the city of Munich: multispectral image (top-left side), panchromatic image (top-right side), TerraSAR-X image (bottom-left side), and fusion of all three images (bottom-right side).

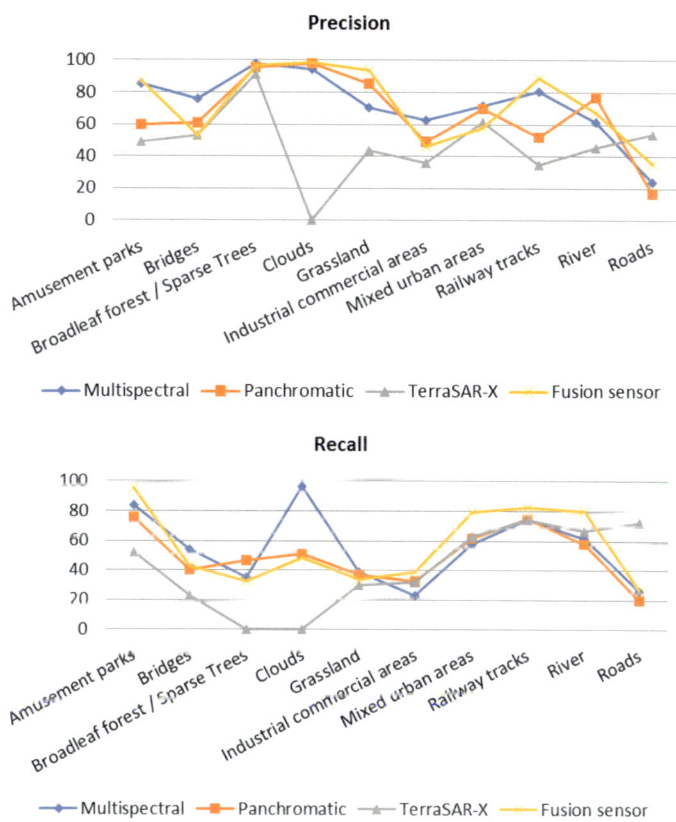

Figure 17.
Classification accuracy (precision/recall) for a selected image over the area of Munich using multispectral, panchromatic, and SAR images and also the fused image.

5. Data science workflows

Recently, a new paradigm for Earth observation, namely, Data Knowledge Discovery, was introduced [17]. This paradigm defines the entire chain "data-information-knowledge-value" and deals with a meaningful EO content extraction, i.e., the semantic and knowledge aspects.

We developed user-invariant and EO domain-specific compensatory methods for the individual user- and domain-subjective biases. The derived models generate a sharable knowledge body as a means to enable the communication between fragmented knowledge learned from metadata, image data, and other data in synergy with the domain expertise of EO users. Today's EO paradigms and technologies are largely domain-oriented and have to support the communication outlined above.

Artificial intelligence big data in Earth observation [13] forced the development of new technologies starting from management platforms [4] and is reaching now the information platforms.

An example for the first category are ESA's Thematic Exploitation Platforms (TEPs) [4] that are designed and focused for coastal applications, forest, geohazards, hydrology, polar, urban, and food and security application domains, integrating standard processing chains that have low user interaction. The Copernicus system (currently still under development) and its data information and access services component [18] are a major achievement but still represent a "classic" management paradigm.

Currently, "classic" existing systems/platforms are usually batch-oriented (e.g., TEPs, DIAS), but with EOLib [20, 40] and the new CANDELA platform [17], this paradigm was "moved" to interactive systems (e.g., supporting active learning).

There are three perspectives to describe this type of interactive systems:

- *The first one is based on signal-information logic* (**Figures 18** and **19**).

The objective is the knowledge extraction from the sensor signal of the physically meaningful parameters or Earth's surface cover categories.

The process is divided in two steps:

- The first step is an automated batch process to manage the satellite image product files, i.e., to extract the image data and to select the relevant metadata, to perform a spatial breakdown of the image into patches, to estimate for each image patch the particular signatures or primitive descriptors, and to further structure the extracted information in a database.

- In a second step following interactive machine learning paradigms, the extracted information is transformed into semantic entities attached to each image location. The process is a combination of querying, browsing, and active learning. Using positive examples, i.e., training samples for the categories of interest and complemented by negative examples to enhance the accuracies of each class, a user can define the image semantics adapted to a particular application.

- *The second perspective is based on the value-adding logic* (**Figure 20**).

Based on these procedures, value-adding is an iterative process.

The satellite data are generally multi-mission data, e.g., multispectral and SAR data that are restructured in a common database, which becomes the **data source**.

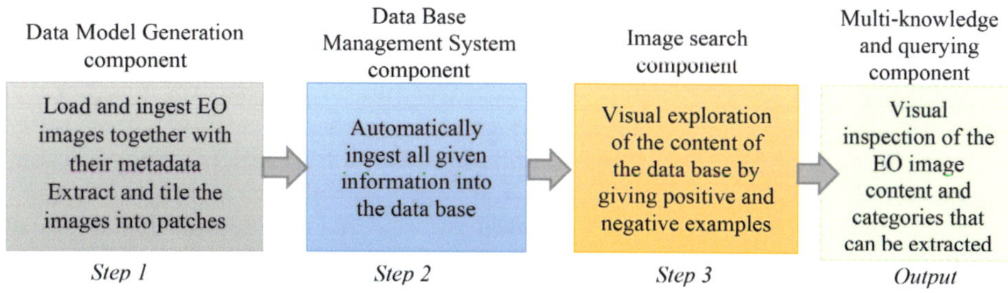

Figure 18.
The signal-information logic scheme: chain → data-information-knowledge.

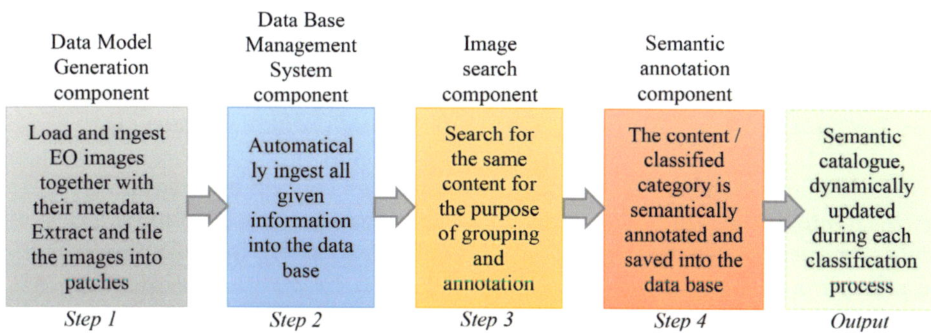

Figure 19.
The signal-information logic scheme: chain → data-information-knowledge-semantic value.

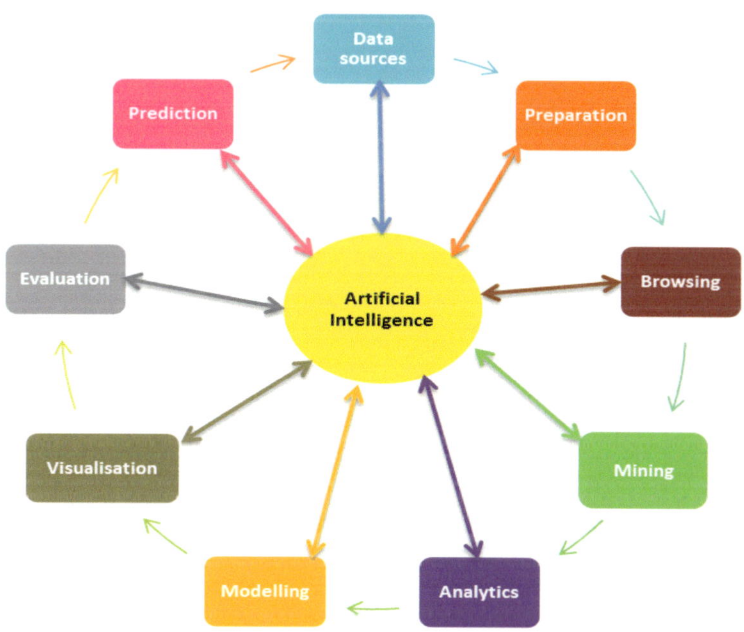

Figure 20.
The value-adding logic scheme.

The **data preparation** component is generating the **Analysis-Ready Data** (ARD) ensuring the least and mandatory processing and organizational steps that enable a direct analysis, thus minimizing the user interaction at the data level.

Among them are the generation of radiometrically and geometrically calibrated data cubes. **Browsing** the data sets is a first step of visual inspection where the user is getting acquainted with the observed structures and their signatures. Further, data mining is an automated process to discover the main data particularities and categories but also detect artifacts or outliers in the data sets, which are beyond the capabilities of human observation, due to the large data volumes and the nonvisual nature of the satellite images. The discovered and selected data sets are further **analyzed** in detail by extracting the particular characteristics of the observed scenes or objects. The results of the analysis are contributing to update existing models or build new models for the observations. **Visualization** of the model parameters or extracted information is a verification step to cope with large complex data volumes. Specific **evaluation** paradigms are needed to build trust in the obtained results, to be used to make **predictions**. The process is iterative, and when new data are acquired, they will be analyzed further.

- *The third perspective is the implementation architecture logic* (**Figure 21**).

The implementation of these paradigms requires a concept of integrating artificial intelligence with software (SW) system architectures enabling interactive multiuser operations in real time relative to the user reaction times. End users will be able to work on shared user scenarios, results of their analyses, or information extraction procedures.

The central component is a **data index (DI)** which is a very specific database model for very fast, real-time management, processing, and distribution of large

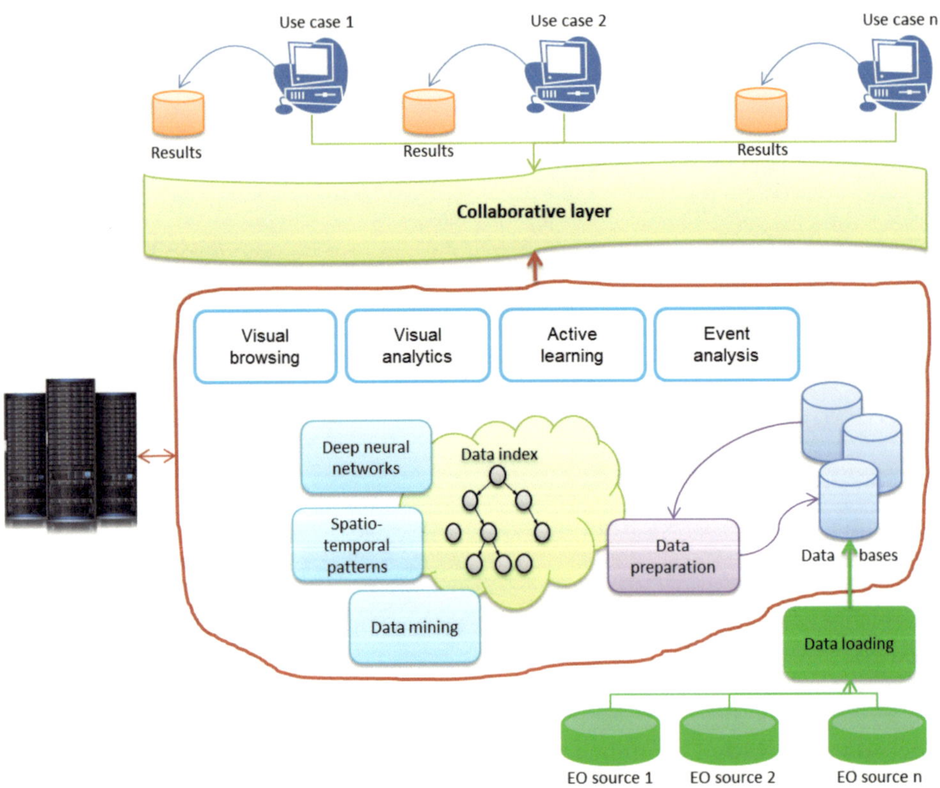

Figure 21.
The logic implementation architecture *scheme.*

structured and unstructured distributed multi-temporal data sets. The data can be efficiently uploaded on demand, coping with large volumes of data from various heterogeneous sources.

The **data preparation** needs to be able to support various tasks for the ARD generation. A **workflow orchestration engine** will be relaying data and offers various processor steps:

- A deep neural network (**DNN module**) for physically meaningful feature learning
- **Spatiotemporal analysis**, e.g., spatiotemporal pattern analysis and extraction for understanding the evolution classes, fusing information from various sources, not just identifying objects, but in particular spatiotemporal patterns and context
- **Data mining** to explore heterogeneous multi-temporal data sets.

The extracted information and data content are again indexed in the DI and provided (via web services) to one of the four human-machine interface (HMI) modules (i.e., **visual browsing, visual analytics, active learning, and event analysis**) supporting advanced big data visualization and active learning paradigms. Once a researcher is satisfied with the results, they can be shared with a restricted group or publically via the **collaborative layer**. These architectures are generically based on federated approaches, making it possible to deploy various components where they fit best, using cloud technologies and web services for communication.

6. Conclusions

The advantages and benefits of the proposed approach are:

- We do clustering considering the physical parameters behind the sensors contrary with the classical classification proposed in AI.
- With very few examples, we are able to classify the images with high accuracy.
- We are able to process multi-sensor data.
- We are able to create a semantic scheme adapted to different EO sensors (SAR or multispectral), high resolution (e.g., TerraSAR X or WorldView)/medium resolution (e.g., Sentinel-1 or Sentinel-2).

7. Future work

During the next years, we expect a wide variety of new satellite image data that can be easily downloaded, handled, and analyzed by individual users. We also think that a number of new geophysical databases and browse tools will become available so that each user has easy access to numerous additional satellite data sources together with auxiliary geophysical data from common libraries and data management tools supporting in-depth image data analyses and their interpretation. Innovative application fields (such as autonomous driving based on machine learning and artificial intelligence) will bring us still more data handling tools and new data archives becoming available via the Internet. In addition, we also suppose that these new tools will be supplemented by management and support environments, for instance, for system testing and performance monitoring. Within the next 5 years, this should result in new established environments for image data understanding.

Acknowledgements

Part of this work was supported by CANDELA—the Copernicus Access Platform Intermediate Layers Small-Scale Demonstrator—a H2020 research and innovation project under grant agreement no. 776193.

Another part of the work was supported by EOLib—the Earth Observation Image Librarian—an ESA technological project.

The TerraSAR-X image data being used in this study were provided by the TerraSAR-X Science Service System (Proposal MTH 1118), while the WorldView-2 image data were provided by the European Space Imaging (EUSI).

Author details

Corneliu Octavian Dumitru[1*], Gottfried Schwarz[1], Fabien Castel[2], Jose Lorenzo[3] and Mihai Datcu[1,4]

1 German Aerospace Center (DLR), Remote Sensing Technology Institute, Wessling, Germany

2 Atos Integration S.A.S (ATOS FR), Toulouse, France

3 Atos Spain S.A. (ATOS ES), Madrid, Spain

4 Politehnica University of Bucharest (UPB), Bucharest, Romania

*Address all correspondence to: corneliu.dumitru@dlr.de

References

[1] Living Planet Symposium. 2019. Available from: http://lps19prog.esa.int/ [Accessed: April 2019]

[2] Lavender S, Lavender A. Practical Handbook of Remote Sensing. Boca Raton: CRC Press; 2015

[3] Reeves RG, Anson A, Landen D, editors. Manual of Remote Sensing. Falls Church, Virgina: American Society of Photogrammetry; 1975

[4] ESA TEPs. 2019. Available from: https://tep.eo.esa.int/ [Accessed: March 2019]

[5] Berger M, Moreno J, Johannessen JA, Hanssen F, Levelt PF, Hannssen RF. ESA's sentinel missions in support of earth system science. Remote Sensing of Environment. 2012;**120**:84-90

[6] ESA Sentinels. 2019. Available from: https://sentinel.esa.int [Accessed: April 2019]

[7] TerraSAR-X. Basic Products Specification Document, Issue: 1.6, TX-GSDD-3302. 2009. Available from: http://sss.terrasar-x.dlr.de/ [Accessed: April 2019]

[8] WorldView. 2019. Available from: https://worldview4.digitalglobe.com [Accessed: April 2019]

[9] ESA Portal. 2019. Available from: https://earth.esa.int/web/eoportal/satellite-missions/t/terrasar-x [Accessed: May 2019]

[10] ESA Sentinel-1 Portal, Geographical Coverage. 2019. Available from: https://sentinel.esa.int/web/sentinel/missions/sentinel-1/satellite-description/geographical-coverage [Accessed: May 2019]

[11] ESA Sentinel-2 Portal, Geographical Coverage. 2019. Available from: https://sentinel.esa.int/web/sentinel/missions/sentinel-2 [Accessed: May 2019]

[12] N2YO. Search Satellite Database. 2018. Available from: https://www.n2yo.com [Accessed: August 2018]

[13] AI4EO Agenda. 2019. Available from: https://eo4society.esa.int/wp-content/uploads/2018/09/ai4eo_v1.0.pdf [Accessed: April 2019]

[14] Datcu M, Dumitru CO, Schwarz G, Castel F, Lorenzo J. Data Science Workflows for the CANDELA Project. 2019. Available from: https://www.bigdatafromspace2019.org [Accessed: April 2019]

[15] Deep Learning. 2019. Available from: https://www.deeplearningbook.org [Accessed: April 2019]

[16] TensorFlow. 2019. Available from: https://www.tensorflow.org [Accessed: March 2019]

[17] CANDELA Project. 2019. Available from: http://www.candela-h2020.eu/ [Accessed: April 2019]

[18] DIAS Platform. 2019. Available from: https://www.copernicus.eu/news/upcoming-copernicus-data-and-information-access-services-dias [Accessed: March 2019]

[19] Dumitru C, Schwarz G, Datcu M. Land cover semantic annotation derived from high-resolution SAR images. The IEEE Journal of Selected Topics in Applied Earth Observations and Remote Sensing. 2018;**11**(5):1571 1592

[20] Earth Observation Image Librarian (EOLib). 2019. Available from: http://wiki.services.eoportal.org/tiki-index.php?page=EOLib [Accessed: April 2019]

[21] Blanchart P, Ferecatu M, Cui S, Datcu M. Pattern retrieval in large

image databases using multiscale coarse-to-fine cascaded active learning. The IEEE Journal of Selected Topics in Applied Earth Observations and Remote Sensing. 2014;7(4):1127-1141

[22] ESA Sentinel-1. 2019. Available from: https://sentinels.copernicus.eu/web/sentinel/missions/sentinel-1 [Accessed: April 2019]

[23] ESA Sentinel-2. 2019. Available from: https://sentinels.copernicus.eu/web/sentinel/missions/sentinel-2 [Accessed: April 2019]

[24] Living Planet Symposium. 2017. Available from: https://lps17.esa.int/ [Accessed: December 2017]

[25] Big Data from Space Conference. 2019. Available from: https://earth.esa.int/web/guest/events/all-events/-/article/conference-on-big-data-from-space-bids-17 [Accessed: April 2019]

[26] IGARSS. 2019. Available from: https://www.igarss2018.org/Tutorials.asp#FD-6 [Accessed: April 2019]

[27] Dumitru CO, Cui S, Datcu MA. Study of multi-sensor satellite image indexing. In: Proceedings of the JURSE 2015. 2019. Available from: http://www.jurse2015.org/program [Accessed: April 2019]

[28] WorldView-2. 2019. Available from: https://www.satimagingcorp.com/satellite-sensors/worldview-2/ [Accessed: April 2019]

[29] Smeulders A, Worring M, Santini S, Gupta A, Jain R. Content-based image retrieval at the end of the early years. IEEE Transactions on Pattern Analysis and Machine Intelligence. 2000;**22**:1349-1380

[30] Torralba A, Russell B, Murphy K, Freeman W. LabelMe: A database and web-based tool for image annotation. International Journal of Computer Vision. 2008;**77**(1-3):157-173

[31] Google. 2019. Available from: https://earthengine.google.com [Accessed: April 2019]

[32] Stepinski T, Netzel P, Jasiewicz J. LandEx-A GeoWeb tool for query and retrieval of spatial patterns in land cover datasets. The IEEE Journal of Selected Topics in Applied Earth Observations and Remote Sensing. 2014;**7**(1):257-266

[33] Shyu CR, Klaric M, Scott G, Barb A, Davis C, Palaniappan K. GeoIRIS: Geospatial information retrieval and indexing system-content mining, semantics modelling, and complex queries. IEEE Transactions on Geoscience and Remote Sensing. 2007;**45**(4):839-852

[34] Boujemaa N. IKONA: Interactive Specific and Generic Image Retrieval. MMCBIR; Glasgow, UK. 2001

[35] Datcu M, Daschiel H, Pelizzari A, Quartulli M, Galoppo A, Colapicchioni A, et al. Information mining in remote sensing image archives: System concepts. IEEE Transactions on Geoscience and Remote Sensing. 2003;**41**(12):2923-2936

[36] TELEIOS Project. 2019. Available from: http://www.earthobservatory.eu [Accessed: April 2019]

[37] Dumitru C, Schwarz G, Datcu M. SAR image land cover datasets for classification benchmarking of temporal changes. The IEEE Journal of Selected Topics in Applied Earth Observations and Remote Sensing. 2018;**11**(5):1571-1592

[38] Orfeo Toolbox an Open Source Collection of Remote Sensing Tools. 2019. Available from: https://www.orfeo-toolbox.org/ [Accessed: February 2019]

[39] ESA Sentinel Toolboxes. 2019. Available from: https://sentinel.esa.int/web/sentinel/toolboxes [Accessed: February 2019]

[40] Espinoza-Molina D, Manilici V, Cui S, Reck CH, Hofmann M, Dumitru CO, et al. Data mining and knowledge discovery for the TerraSAR-X payload ground segment. In: Proceedings of the PV 2015, Darmstadt, Germany. 2015

[41] Knowledge-based Information Mining (KIM). 2019. Available from: https://wiki.services.eoportal.org/tiki-index.php?page=KIM+Project [Accessed: April 2019]